HAUNTED
ELKHART
COUNTY

HAUNTED ELKHART COUNTY

MARK P. DODDINGTON

Haunted America

Published by Haunted America
A Division of The History Press
Charleston, SC
www.historypress.com

First published 2022

Manufactured in the United States

ISBN 9781467150934

Library of Congress Control Number: 2022937893

For Jim, Pat, Andrew and Evan.

CONTENTS

Preface   9
Author's Note   15

1. A Murderous Murder Victim: Benton Lutheran Cemetery,
   Benton   17
2. Meeting of the Minds: Charles Hall, Bristol   19
3. Part of the Family: Cathcart-Burke House, Bristol   24
4. The Town That Never Was: Bonneyville Mill, Bristol   31
5. The House of Many Sorrows: Milburn House, Bristol   34
6. Not to His Taste: Solomon Fowler Mansion, Bristol   39
7. Where History Lives On: Washington Township High School,
   Bristol   44
8. Noises Off: Bristol Opera House, Bristol   49
9. The House by the Town Burying Ground: Cusimano Residence,
   Bristol   53
10. The Past Is Present: Simonton House, Elkhart   57
11. "When the Last One Lets You Go": Wilson Wilbert Wilt House,
    Elkhart   64
12. The Only Place He Felt Safe: Samuel Strong School, Elkhart   73
13. Nice Place for a Picnic: Grace Lawn Cemetery, Elkhart   77
14. All Good Things Must Come to an End…Even Robbie:
    Century Club, Elkhart   84
15. To the Manor Born: South Residence, Elkhart   87

16. A Nurse's Duty Never Ends: Clark Street Hospital, Elkhart   90
17. The House That Nellie Built...and Never Left:
     Winchester Mansion, Elkhart   94
18. Where Dreams Come True...Maybe: Lerner Theater,
     Elkhart   106
19. Where the Spirits Have a Ball: State Farm Office, Goshen   109
20. That Ol' School Spirit: Umble Hall, Goshen College,
     Goshen   116
21. Night Shift: The Old Bag Factory, Goshen   118
22. The Man in the Red Flannel Shirt: Elkhart County Jail,
     Goshen   123
23. A Hole in Space and Time: Elkhart County Home,
     Ox Bow Park, Goshen   128
24. Four Stories, No Answers: Cable Line Road, Jimtown   131
25. The Crying Stone: Union Center Cemetery, near Nappanee   135

Conclusion   139
About the Author   141

PREFACE

Back in the early 1990s, there was a short-lived TV series titled *Eerie, Indiana*, which chronicled the fictional spooky events in a small midwestern town. The show depicted the little hamlet as rife with paranormal activity. While Indiana does have its share of claims of the weird and wondrous, they do not appear distributed equally across the map. Of the ninety-two counties in Indiana, heavily populated Elkhart County seems to be among the least haunted—or most tight-lipped—in the state. Doing research for this book proved challenging, as very few ghosts, monsters, UFOs or urban legends claimed roots in this county of more than two hundred thousand souls (living, that is). Even the Elkhart Lake Monster lives in Wisconsin!

I'm not sure I understand the reticence, if indeed that's what it is, to talk about the paranormal. It could be religious, I suppose. Southern Elkhart County has a high Amish population, which may contribute to the reluctance. I admit I am not well versed in Amish thinking regarding the supernatural. I understand that they do believe in ghosts but are generally unwilling to discuss the topic, particularly with outsiders. I was raised Methodist, largely because of my father, and the subject of ghosts was not encouraged. Nor was it actively discouraged, I must add in all fairness. But I do know that my father was not keen on the matter. Then again, he and I never did see eye to eye on matters of religion.

I have always had an open mind on the subject of ghosts. In fact, I devour the subject. I can still recall the exact moment I became hooked.

My mother returned from a trip to her native England in 1978 with a book by Peter Underwood titled *A Gazetteer of Scottish and Irish Ghosts* (London, Harrap, 1973). I was about ten years old when I found that book in her apartment one weekend. I picked it up and could not put it down! It scared the hell out of me with its straightforward, almost clinical style. There was no "it was a dark and stormy night," flowery prose to enable me to dismiss it as mere fiction. (Yes, I thought about this sort of thing when I was ten.) There was no mistaking that this book was pure fact. Only many years later did I learn that there is nothing to fear from ghosts. After all, they're simply people who are no longer alive in their physical bodies. And let's face it, today's world is a lot scarier on *this* side of the veil than it is on the other. Anyway, I've read that book at least twenty times and have been hooked on the subject ever since.

When I moved to Michigan in 2010, I had the opportunity to join a ghost-hunting team, T~NIPS (The Northern Indiana Paranormal Society). After a few years, I formed my own team, SPEAR (Stateline Paranormal Exploration and Research). Sadly, neither team is still afloat, for various reasons. But the love of the Unknown has always had an allure for me, ever since I read that tome. In fact, I deliberately purchased an old Victorian in White Pigeon, Michigan, in the hopes that it would prove to be haunted.

I got my wish. That house, an Italianate built in 1876 for local entrepreneur and philanthropist Benjamin Fieldhouse and his wife, Mary Anne, was very active. I believe it harbored at least four spirits, including that of my late cat, Midnyte, who had traveled with me from home to home ever since she died in 2006 back in Milwaukee. She has since moved on, I think, as I no longer feel her jumping up on the bed each night.

I hated losing that house to foreclosure, but I must admit I love Elkhart, Indiana. I now live in another old house (the 1903 Wilson Wilbert Wilt House—gotta love that name!), which has provided its own serving of unexplained happenings, detailed in this book.

Let's look at the facts: As we all know, a ghost is commonly believed to be the soul, spirit, energy (call it what you will) of a person who has died. That person had a life. That life is part of history. We pursue the paranormal for a number of reasons, one of which is a love of history. To make contact with a spirit, all too rare an event, is to learn about the past, not to mention gaining a possible taste of one's own future. As for me, I am undecided whether I want to come back as a ghost. If I did, I don't know if I'd want to stay that way for eternity. But it might be fun for a while. Besides, where would I choose to haunt, assuming I had the choice?

Which brings up an interesting point: Are ghosts aware of their surroundings or the passing of time? Some people believe they are; others disagree. It might depend on the type of haunting in question. Anyone who has studied the subject is aware that there are at least three basic types of haunting. An intelligent haunting involves a spirit that is actively trying to communicate with the living world for one purpose or another, perhaps to complete an unfinished task before moving on to a higher plane. Such ghosts will go to great lengths to attract your attention: slamming doors, walking on creaky floors, touching, talking or showing themselves. They want something from you. Don't worry, it's usually harmless. So-called shadow people and Doppelgängers (a person's "evil twin") are similar.

Another type of haunting is called residual. The common belief is that energy generated by a great emotional event imprints itself on the environment—stone walls, a cherished piece of furniture, even the land itself. This energy then repeatedly replays, like a recording on a loop, and sensitive people and equipment can detect it under the right conditions. Such a haunting is not aware of its surroundings and merely repeats with no more consciousness than a flower turning toward the sun.

The third major type of haunting is the dreaded Poltergeist, from the German for "noisy ghost." Such nasty spirits—if spirits they be—are renowned for their destructive nature. Anything from throwing stones and household objects to starting fires and inflicting physical torture on one or more living victims—the Poltergeist knows no bounds. One commonly but not universally accepted theory is that a Poltergeist is actually a form of telekinesis, the mind's ability to move objects without physical contact. Such cases are often experienced in the home of an adolescent in the throes of puberty. The belief is that these changes, so confusing to the teenage body, generate malevolent, though usually unbidden, energy that can lash out in many directions, even focusing on a particular individual. In such cases, it is believed that the adolescent in question has no idea what is happening and has no control over it or what the alleged spirit chooses to do with this power.

Another category of haunting does not truly qualify as a haunting at all. Demons, usually regarded as malevolent beings (though this is not always the case) that never resided on earth in corporeal form, lie well beyond the realm of ghosts, falling more in the category of theology and, thus, distinctly beyond the scope of this book.

What does any of this have to do with you? Well, you picked up this book, so you clearly have some interest in the paranormal or in local history, or another factor enticed you to begin reading it. Perhaps you're merely curious about life after death. Maybe you'd like to become a paranormal investigator yourself. Perhaps you've had an experience you can't explain or can't even share and are simply looking for someone who understands. (Statistics vary from survey to survey, but they show that at any given time at least fifty percent of Americans believe in ghosts and the supernatural.) Or maybe, just maybe, you want to have the crap scared out of you by seeking out these dark places. Fear does play a valuable part in the human psyche. These are all valid reasons and are nothing you should be embarrassed about. But I must caution you: Some of the places described in this book are private property. You should make every effort to obey local laws regarding access and be respectful of an owner's right to privacy. Just because someone has chosen to speak to me about their experiences doesn't mean they'll welcome strangers at their door asking nosy questions. Think about how you would feel if you were the one dealing with a haunting, and act accordingly. The same rule applies to public places. Respect those who live or work there now, respect those who linger after death and, please, respect the environment. Don't turn the local cemetery into a party spot because you think it might be a thrill. Would you want people dumping trash on your grave? I didn't think so.

Before we go behind the scenes, so to speak, let's talk a little about the history of Elkhart County. To begin, the territory that would become the State of Indiana was settled by Native Americans, most notably the Chippewa, Ottawa and Potawatomi Nations around eight thousand years ago. European settlers, predominantly of English, Irish and German descent, began moving into the area in the 1700s, forming settlements throughout the territory between Lake Michigan and the Ohio River. Indiana became the nineteenth state, admitted to the union on December 11, 1816.

The completion of the Erie Canal in 1821 and the subsequent end of the Blackhawk War in 1832 brought a surge of migration from New York and New England, rapidly increasing the population of the Midwest and shifting the ethnic demographics. Although there was some hostility between Native Americans and the newcomers, substantial harmony existed as well. Indeed, Dr. Havilah Beardsley of Connecticut, founder of the City of Elkhart, formed a lifelong friendship with Potawatomi chief Pierre Moran, himself the son of a French fur trader.

Elkhart County was officially established on April 1, 1830. Its seat was the town of Dunlap. Shortly after, adjustments were made to the county borders, encompassing the present 468 square miles, and the seat was moved to the more centrally located town of Goshen.

There are several unverified stories regarding the county's name. One story claims that the county was named after the Elkhart tribe. Unfortunately for the author of this tale, there is no evidence that such a tribe existed. The most romantic tale suggests that the name came from the shape of the island in Island Park (in downtown Elkhart), but airborne transport was in its infancy at the time. Hot-air balloons were in existence, but it is doubtful that they could have flown high enough for anyone to determine the shape of the island. A third story, the most likely of the three, is that the county was named after Shawnee chief Elkhart, a cousin of the legendary Tecumseh. My own theory is much more prosaic and based on my knowledge of the English language. An elk is a deer. A hart is a male deer. Thus, someone may have spied a male elk (an elk hart—note the spelling), thus affixing the name, intentionally or not, to the region. Like the other theories, however, this is pure speculation.

In any case, eight millennia of human habitation have clearly left its mark on this small square of land along the Michigan border. It stands to reason that some of that energy has imprinted itself on the rocks, roads, buildings and memories of the region.

It is important to note that some of the stories in this book are better documented than others. Some, such as that of the Cable Line Road

Map of Elkhart County.

Monster, barely qualify as anything more than urban legend, while others, such as the Bristol Opera House, have had many witnesses over the years. Some have been covered by the media; many are printed here for the first time. As a result, some of these stories are quite short compared to others. Save for those I have investigated or experienced firsthand, I cannot vouch for any of them as authentic. I consider myself a skeptical believer. I believe in ghosts, but I don't take everyone's story as gospel.

In addition, record-keeping before the age of computers was sporadic. Many documents, particularly prior to the twentieth century, contradict each other, as is noted throughout this book. Therefore, some of the dates cited may, on further research, prove incorrect. Nevertheless, the stories themselves are what count, and they are fascinating.

All that being said, sit in a darkened room with just a small light to illuminate this book, turn off the TV, silence your phone and sink into the shadows. Keep an eye and an ear open to the environment while you read, just in case someone is reaching out to you from the Beyond.

AUTHOR'S NOTE

In talking with people for this book, I made a point of guaranteeing anonymity to anyone who requested it. For those people, I have changed their names. Such individuals are identified by an asterisk (*) the first time their "name" appears in the text. Similarly, I have omitted addresses of private homes or businesses whose owners choose to remain anonymous.

All photos in this book were taken by me unless otherwise noted.

On another note, I would like to thank the following people for their assistance in putting this book together. First and foremost, to John Rodrigue at Arcadia Press / The History Press, for giving me this wonderful opportunity. Next, to Marcia VanZile, dear friend and co-homeowner, for tagging along, both literally and figuratively, on this journey. To RoseMary McDaniel, Penny Hayes*, Betty Qualls*, and Linda Fiske*, otherwise known in Bristol as the "Story Tellers." And to all of the people who shared their stories and their trust.

To the entire Ruthmere staff for their support, assistance and encouragement. In particular, Jennifer Johns, curator, for passing on John Rodrigue's email, and Andrea "Dree" Barbour, outreach curator, for proofreading the manuscript for me.

To Bryan Telsworth, Rachel Polosky and Geoff Walkling of T~NIPS, and to Jesse and Matie James of SPEAR, for allowing me to use their cases.

And I want to give a special callout to Ruth Rockwell, docent at Ruthmere Museum, who put me in contact with the Story Tellers and really got the ball rolling full tilt. Ruth, I owe you a big bottle of very expensive champagne!

1

A Murderous Murder Victim

Benton Lutheran Cemetery, Benton

Like many cemeteries around the world, tiny Benton Lutheran Cemetery in southern Elkhart County has its own resident ghost— nameless, unauthenticated, ambiguous.

Situated near the crossroads of U.S. 33 and State Road 44 in the rural hamlet of Benton, this cemetery, one and a half acres in size, was founded on October 11, 1847, when Martin and Barbara Vance gave property for its inception. Approximately four hundred graves hold the cemetery's occupants. The nearby Lutheran church, half a mile away, was sold to the Mennonite community some years ago.

There are two accounts of the ghost of Benton Lutheran, and they disagree only on the human identity of the specter. Some people believe he was a local recluse, others that he was a caretaker at the cemetery in the 1880s. Both accounts agree that the man was beaten to death with a large club of some sort by a band of ruffians in search of a cache of gold the old man had supposedly buried in the grounds of the graveyard.

Whoever he may have been, his ghost is said to loom out of the darkness, ten feet tall, brandishing a club, maybe even the one used to murder him somewhere in the mists of time. Recorded details of the haunting are sketchy and infrequent. The earliest written account comes from a Mennonite couple in the 1890s that encountered the specter while driving their buggy past the cemetery at night.

As with many ghost stories, this one may be no more than an urban legend—an Irving-esque tale of a vengeful fiend seeking retribution for the wrong done him more than a century ago. With no hard evidence to back it up, the story must remain a folktale meant to scare children around a campfire. Maybe you should check it out for yourself. Take a video camera— and a pith helmet, just in case.

2
MEETING OF THE MINDS

RoseMary McDaniel is a Bristol historian and author and a friend of Ruth Rockwell, a Ruthmere docent who put the two of us in touch. RoseMary, whose books include *Murder at the Museum & Other Fruithills Suspense Stories* and *Beckoning Bonneyville Mill & Other Fruithills Suspense Stories Vol. 2*, is the owner of Charles Hall, a house built by Thomas Hilbish in 1875.

Thomas was born on April 1, 1842, in Juniata County, Pennsylvania, the third of five children born to Peter and Katherine Beckhart Hilbish. Peter and Katherine, both of German descent, relocated to Washington Township, Elkhart County, in 1846 or 1856 (documents conflict).

Thomas was educated in Bristol, learned in the arts of farming, and lived with his father until he was twenty-three. At that time, setting his sights on a more gentlemanly lifestyle, he set himself up in business in Bristol, opening a general store with partners William C. Birch and Andrew Aiken. W.C. Birch & Company prospered for three years before its namesake decided to retire. The business was renamed Hilbish & Company. Aiken retired in 1880, leaving Thomas as the sole proprietor of the store. He built the house on Charles Street in 1875.

In 1875 or 1878 (again, records differ), Thomas married Emma J. Walter, herself a Pennsylvania native born in 1852. They settled on Charles Street, creating a home for the three children who would eventually arrive: Clyde, Myron and Florence. In later years, Thomas served as treasurer of the town of Bristol and, with his two sons, ran the Bristol State Bank. He owned additional land in the countryside surrounding Bristol. He passed away at the house on Charles Street on February 16, 1918, at the age of seventy-five, a victim of heart disease, and was laid to rest in Oak Ridge Cemetery in Bristol.

Clyde Hilbish, the eldest of his children, was born on March 31, 1879. He married Ada M. Sherwin in 1903. (Ada was the daughter of Richard Sherwin, RoseMary's great-uncle.) They had a daughter, Clara, on January 8, 1907. Clara lived in the family home

Thomas Hilbish, builder of Charles Hall.

until she married William H. Dubois and set up house in Bristol. Ada Hilbish passed away on October 25, 1947. Clyde followed her on October 21, 1962, almost fifteen years to the day. Clara passed away in 1985 at the age of seventy-eight. Clyde and Ada are buried at Cathcart Cemetery behind the old high school, now the Elkhart County Historical Society. The remaining family members, including Clara, are interred at Oak Ridge Cemetery in Bristol. Cathcart Cemetery itself is allegedly haunted by the ghost of a Revolutionary War soldier.

Charles Hall, situated on Charles Street and so named by RoseMary, has served a variety of purposes in its lifetime, including a funeral home starting in the early twentieth century. By 1978, the mortuary had ceased preparing bodies on-site and was doing funeral services only. RoseMary and her husband, Carl, purchased the house in 2005 and converted it back into a private home. It also houses the McDaniel Library, RoseMary's personal collection of books and documents covering almost every aspect of Elkhart County history, as well as the mortuary's records for several decades. A variety of personal items from her father and grandfather add cheerful ambience to her home, including a blackthorn shillelagh her grandfather brought over from Ireland.

RoseMary and her friends Penny Hayes*, Betty Qualls* and Linda Fiske* are known locally as the "Story Tellers," keepers of the history of Bristol and the surrounding area extending well beyond the borders of Elkhart County.

"One of the things when I had a group come of paranormal people," RoseMary says, "and they went down there and they said—this is before

Charles Hall, where the original owner's granddaughter still hangs out.

we tore down some walls—that used to be a porch and we made it into a restroom. In that corner," RoseMary says as she points to an area of negative space above the downstairs bathroom door, "the spirits here would gather and they would kind of hang out around there. But if there's too much noise going on here, they would go out to the carriage house, which was their second preferred place to go.

"I personally have never seen them or anything," continues RoseMary, "but Penny has had an experience, Betty had an experience here. So I think they are here."

Betty Qualls, a retired nurse whose parents were both quite psychic and whose father was laid out at Charles Hall during its days as Stemm-Lawson Funeral Parlor, talked about an encounter she had upstairs in what is now RoseMary's living room (once the casket showroom). "There was a lady sitting in the chair, and she turned around and looked over the back of the chair. Kind of startled me. I said, 'Oh, I'm so sorry.' I said, 'Hi, I'm Betty, and I'm in the meeting with RoseMary downstairs,' and she doesn't say anything. So I went downstairs and I said, 'RoseMary, you didn't tell me you had company, you know, this young lady sitting up there and I scared the hell out of her!'"

RoseMary informed her that there was no one upstairs, but Betty insisted. Examining photographs of the previous residents of the house, Betty discovered an exact likeness: Clara Hilbish! She appeared as a young woman, as she may have looked in the 1920s. Apparently, however, she has not been seen since. "I'm maybe not paying enough attention," RoseMary says, "or they don't like me, I don't know."

One of the more unusual aspects of the friendship between Betty Qualls and RoseMary McDaniel is the fact that they lived across the street from each other in Elkhart for several years and never knew it. Only after they had both relocated, independently, to Bristol did they come to meet and learn of the odd connection they share.

At the time, RoseMary lived in the Simonton House now occupied by Jim and Carol Reeves (read their story in chapter 10), and Betty lived directly across on the other side of Cassopolis Street. Betty spoke of a dream she once had that the previous owner of her home had died and was laid out in the house. The woman sat up and told Betty, "Don't cry. We don't really die." The next day, Betty learned that the woman had actually passed away elsewhere.

The woman's brother had committed suicide in Betty's house many years earlier. Betty's daughter would eventually occupy the room in which he died.

"She would not sleep in her room," Betty recalls. "She would wake up in the night and come sneaking in our bed. She had this imaginary playmate and she described him as a grown man, an old man. I forget his name, Oscar or whatever it was. And I thought, you don't make up a name like that. She would blame lots of things on Oscar and said, 'I don't like it when Oscar comes in and looks at me at night. It scares me.' That imaginary playmate was a real person, a ghost!"

Penny recalls the first time she went down into the basement at Charles Hall. She and RoseMary were inspecting the bizarre arrangements of pipes, including several valves placed at oddly low positions, almost on the floor. At first Penny could not figure out the purpose of having valves at such an awkward height. Finally it dawned on her. That was where the morticians prepped the bodies for funeral services, and those valves most likely facilitated the draining away of blood during the embalming process. Needless to say, she was chilled by the thought. Although she experienced nothing of a paranormal nature, she nevertheless beat a hasty retreat upstairs!

We moved upstairs, where Betty had encountered the spirit of Clara Hilbish. We had two options for getting up to RoseMary's apartment: the main stairs or…The Elevator. Naturally, I opted for the more interesting choice, especially after hearing RoseMary describe it. The elevator actually consists of a wall-less platform on a vertical track, very shaky and completely exposed.

"A lot of people are afraid of it," Penny laughs, to which RoseMary heartily agrees.

"I was afraid of it at first, actually," RoseMary adds. She explains that the elevator went to all four levels of the building and was used to transport caskets and bodies to wherever they were needed. Because of its unnerving personality, she admits, she was compelled to add side panels to keep people from feeling as if they were about to tumble into the embalming room and become corpses themselves.

It wasn't as nerve-wracking as it sounds, though the platform does shudder as it moves, propelled by a motor with a banshee-like scream that does nothing to assuage one's fears.

In RoseMary's living room, Penny points out the easy chair where Clara was resting at the time of Betty's encounter. It is a very modern chair, the likes of which a young Clara Hilbish had probably never seen. This brings up a question: Did Clara "see" the room as it appeared when she was young?

A chance discovery a week later revealed to me that RoseMary's maiden name was Sherwin. "I had no idea that I was connected to [Charles Hall]," she writes in an email, "so it was not why I bought it. My husband wanted to live in Bristol and so did I. And the house came up for sale at the right time. I didn't know anything about my great uncle Richard and [aunt] Ada until I moved here and started researching Bristol history and obits. Odd, isn't it?"

On a later visit with RoseMary and Penny, the latter recounted smelling smoke in the main meeting room at Charles Hall, even though no one was smoking in the house and no one had smoked in that room since RoseMary acquired the old funeral home. During that visit, Penny also saw a shadow pass behind RoseMary. No one else saw it, and no cars were driving up or down Charles Street at the time, so its source remains a mystery.

3
PART OF THE FAMILY

CATHCART-BURKE HOUSE, BRISTOL

The house has been in some part of my family since 1883. I was born there. I'm the seventh generation in town." So says, with justified pride, Catherine Cathcart Burke, of the slate-blue house on Vistula Street in Bristol, just a couple blocks from RoseMary's house on Charles.

"My daughter, when she was twelve," Cathy says, "when my mother was living, she put fifty cents on her television and said, 'That's a down-payment on the house.' Well, I got it next and she didn't! She only lives two doors down from me. She visits all the time."

It would seem this venerable house, constructed in 1853, still anchors many generations of the Cathcart family. The Cathcarts were one of the founding families of Bristol, Indiana. James and Prenina Leonard Cathcart relocated from the Philadelphia area in 1831 and purchased much of the land in what is now Bristol, including the tracts where the post office and high school–cum–history museum stand today. In fact, the tiny cemetery behind the museum, reputedly haunted by the ghost of a Revolutionary War soldier buried on the riverbank just outside the fenced-in area, is named Cathcart Cemetery. Only about ten graves lie within the fence—ten *marked* graves—but dowsing revealed many more in the surrounding area.

One year before settling in town, James and Prenina had a son named Ira, born on September 20, 1830. They also had two daughters, Flora

Cathcart-Burke house, home of one of Bristol's founding families.

and Oranda, one of whom was mentally ill. As adults, the sisters shared a house on family land behind the current post office. Neither ever married.

James Cathcart passed away in 1839, when Ira was only eight, leaving Prenina to handle the family's business affairs. Unfortunately, this would prove disastrous for the family, through no fault of her own. Ira enlisted in the army in 1861 and fought in the Civil War, being discharged in 1865 when the war ended. While he was away, Prenina was confronted with a tax demand for $3.79, which she was unable to pay. The government seized large tracts of the family's sixty-five acres. The portion where Cathy's house stands was spared.

Ira married Savilla Sturner of Schuylkill, Pennsylvania, in the 1850s and purchased the house on Vistula Street in 1883, adding the front extension to the house at that time. They had two daughters, Ada and Nora. Ira died on May 6, 1888, though several records list an unspecified date in 1870. Savilla followed on July 6, 1913. Neither Ada nor Nora married, both dying in the 1940s. They are buried next to each other in Oak Ridge Cemetery in Bristol.

The timeline of ownership becomes very murky at this point. After at least one other owner, Cathy's aunt Charlotte "Lottie" and uncle William

Artley acquired the house about 1932. Lottie Menges Artley passed away in 1953. She and Will never had children, so the house eventually passed to Cathy's mother and then to Cathy and her husband.

If a house can retain the spirits of past family members, then the Cathcart house is a veritable hotel of haunts. According to Cathy, at least four of her loved ones still dwell with her. "My daughter moved into there when my mother passed away with her young son, and came and asked me one day. She said, 'Who's the man with the butch haircut?' She'd never met my father. And I said, 'Where did you see him? And who are you talking about?' She said he was standing at the top of the stairs. And I said, 'That's my father.'"

Ironically, Cathy does not remember her father ever going upstairs, although he did remodel a bedroom up there, putting up sheet rock to turn one room into two. When Cathy moved back into the house as an adult, she recalls removing some of the drywall to ensure that the walls had been properly insulated. Inside the wall, she discovered some of her father's tools, as well as a sterling silver fork of her mother's that Cathy is sure she herself placed there as a mischievous six-year-old.

Further, she remembers how fastidious her father was about his tools, always making sure to put them back exactly where they belonged. She tells of the time she was using her father's hammer to repair some loose shingles on her roof. Her daughter Lisa was working with her, using a separate hammer. When rain threatened their enterprise, Cathy decided to take a break until the storm passed. They laid their hammers side by side in the garage and went inside. Once the rain subsided, they returned to their task. However, only one hammer—the newer one—was present. She and Lisa searched for her father's old hammer, eventually finding it in the basement, exactly where her father kept it during his lifetime. "That was my dad," she says emphatically.

That's one family member inhabiting the home after their death.

Cathy points out a smoke detector in her home. She says it has never given her a day's trouble. However, there are times when the device will give an uncharacteristic three blinks as Cathy passes by. She attributes this to her mother saying good night and is always ready to offer a response in kind!

Her mother had made her living room in the front part of the house (the 1883 addition), where Cathy now displays most of her antiques. Cathy's living room, on the other hand, is toward the back of the house, and the front room is no longer set up for that purpose.

Stairway, Cathcart-Burke house, where Cathy's father's ghost was seen.

"That's where she had her television and everything. I have looked down the hall at night and seen a shadow walk across that living room. I know it was my mother. She looked like a little barrel." That's an apt description, according to Cathy.

That's two family members.

"I was dating somebody for about three years," she continues.

Don passed away about three and a half, four years ago. My granddaughter, Mary, and Don were inseparable. They had that connection that nobody else has. He was gonna teach her to drive when she was sixteen. So they made a pact where he was gonna take her up into Michigan to drive on different roads and highways and all this stuff. Well, that never came through. We didn't know that until after he died.

Well, the day he died was the day of her prom. He was in hospice, and she was so afraid because she promised he would see her in her dress. So we went to hospice. She sat at the end of his bed. He was at the point where he hadn't said anything for a day or two. I said, "Mary, why not put your dress on?" So she put her dress on and she came out. He turned his head, he looked at her, and went [Cathy clicks her tongue and makes a gun gesture] *and that was the only thing he had done all day. After he died, she would go out to his property and sit where we used to have bonfires for hours and just sit there. And she said, "Nana, I knew he was there."*

Cathy is convinced that Don is still in her house. Naturally, when she and he were dating, Don spent a lot of time at the house on Vistula Street. She recalled how he once teased her about her refrigerator light going off and her asking him to fix it. He took one quick look inside, tightened the bulb and told her it would never happen again. Periodically, her refrigerator light will blink out momentarily when it shouldn't. She believes Don is still making fun of her technical lapse.

That's three.

During a conversation on the front porch at Charles Hall a week or so before, Penny Hayes asked if Cathy had ever sensed the presence of any of her ancestors in the house. Cathy was quick with a reply:

My Aunt Lottie. Well, her name was Charlotte [Menges Artley]. *Her mother passed away when she was eight. My mother moved in with Aunt Lottie and Uncle Will, into my house. After Uncle Will died, Aunt Lottie became blind—she had diabetes. And my mother told me that from the time I was born 'til I was two years old, [Lottie] rocked me. And I still, once in a while, will see the chair move. It's not my cats, I can tell you that. I usually attribute it to truck traffic on the highway. 'Course, I live right on the highway. But…you don't know. So you take it for what you think it is. And I still think it's Aunt Lottie.*

That's four.

The fact that she blames traffic while at the same time crediting Charlotte Artley with rocking the chair is common among many people confronted with alleged paranormal activity. It's only natural that one would try to explain away such things, particularly if they are not prepared to accept the possibility of a ghost in their lives. Rationalization can be comforting. However, Cathy claims that paranormal experiences are commonplace in her family and thus a natural part of life.

She also believes her late cat Prissy is in the house. She claims that she will hear the distinct sound of four furry feet coming down the creaky stairs, even when her current cats are already downstairs and accounted for.

So that makes five! If she ever decides to charge the ghosts rent, she'll make a fortune.

Cathy also recounts her efforts at redecorating the house, inside and out. She always remembered the house being a dark bluish-gray. After her father died, her mother decided to repaint the house in what Cathy describes as "baby-poop light green." She also recalls picking out wallpaper for the upstairs and discovering a patch of wallpaper hidden behind an old radiator—identical to what she had chosen.

"Don't tell me that was my own idea. I think somebody said, you know, 'This is the way it originally was.' And then I got to thinking, 'Well, why did you paint the house baby-poop green?'"

She has since repainted the house the bluish-gray of her memories.

Perhaps the most bizarre incident occurred on July 18, 2019. Cathy points out the alley that runs between her house and the daycare center next door. Previously, she had noticed that the tree in the daycare's front yard had a fungus growth around the base that had attacked the roots, thereby weakening the tree. Cathy recalls leaving for work around 7:45 a.m. on the morning of July 18 and arriving just before the hour. Almost immediately after entering work, before she even had a chance to punch in, her daughter informed her that the tree had fallen and smashed through Cathy's upstairs wall! Needless to say, she was shocked.

"The tree was in my house, this big around." She holds up her arms in a wide circle. "Knocked the bookshelf over. Windows gone. Part of my slate roof's gone." She contemplates the unthinkable. What if she'd still been home? What if her grandkids were visiting? It is too horrible to consider.

Answering Penny's query as to whether she thinks this evoked any paranormal activity, Cathy says, again emphatically, "Yes! You know, not to the worst. I felt comfort, I did feel that my whole family was there. All I feel is security in that house. It's always been that way."

4

THE TOWN THAT NEVER WAS

BONNEYVILLE MILL, BRISTOL

Industrial accidents have been a fact of workaday life since before the Industrial Revolution. In the early days of America, before the enactment of child labor laws, young children frequently worked in mills and factories, often in some of the most dangerous jobs to be had. Their small hands were ideal for wiggling into the guts of heavy machinery to untangle knots and snags. Their status as minors, and thus as the "property" of their parents—who often sent them to do these hazardous tasks for a pittance— meant that many factory and mill owners felt no sense of responsibility for their welfare. Days were long and monotonous, and workers' compensation was unheard of. As a result, accidents on the job involving both children and adults were a matter of course.

Bonneyville Mill, situated in Bonneyville Mill County Park on County Road 131 between Bristol and Middlebury, is no exception. Built in 1837 (though the building itself bears the date 1832) on the Little Elkhart River, Bonneyville Mill is the oldest gristmill in Indiana still in use. To this day, it produces flour ground on its two massive millstones.

Edward Bonney was born on August 26, 1807, in Essex County, New York, the son of Jethro Bonney and Laurana Webster. Edward married Maria L. Van Frank in Homer, New York, on January 17, 1832. A little more than a year later, they set their sights on a new life in the young state of Indiana. Over the next several years, they had four children: Eliza, Mary Elizabeth, Martha and William Edward.

Bonneyville Mill, haunted by several ghosts.

Bonney established his mill on the Little Elkhart River in the expectation that a thriving community would grow around it. Fueled by dreams of a canal or a railroad passing the mill, Bonney set about building his empire. Alas, neither form of transportation would grace Bonneyville Mill, and Edward's dreams of a town bearing his name never came to fruition. The mill, however, continued to thrive.

Unsubstantiated reports of Edward Bonney being arrested for counterfeiting tell of his fleeing Indiana for Nauvoo, Illinois, in 1842, where he befriended Mormon leader Joseph Smith. Later records show Bonney living in nearby Lee County, Iowa.

During his time on the Mississippi shores, Bonney pursued a career as a bounty hunter. He published a book in 1850, *The Banditti of the Prairies, or The Murderers' Doom!! A Tale of the Mississippi Valley*. The book, which tells of his exploits in tracking desperadoes and fugitives in the mid-1840s, has been reprinted several times. In it, Bonney tells of his arrests, once for murder and once for counterfeiting. The murder charge never came to court due to a lack of evidence, and the counterfeiting charge was dismissed by a jury, a result, according to Bonney, of his friendship with the governor of Illinois.

By 1860, Bonney was living in Chicago and still working as a bounty hunter. He enlisted in the 127th Illinois Infantry, Company G, on October 22, 1862, at the age of fifty-five, serving in the Union army during the Civil War. His talents as a bounty hunter guided him in his military work, tracking and retrieving deserters from the Union army. Bonney served only a few months in the army before receiving a disability discharge on December 23, 1863. Less than two months later, he died in Chicago, on February 4, 1864. He is reportedly buried in Bonneyville Cemetery, where a memorial stone bears his name. No cemetery records exist to support or refute this.

Originally powered by water, the mill was converted to electricity in 1919 and restored in 1970 as the core of Bonneyville Mill County Park. In 1976, the mill was added to the National Register of Historic Places.

According to RoseMary McDaniel in her book *Beckoning Bonneyville Mill & Other Fruithills Mysteries*, the mill is said to be haunted by the ghost of a young miller, aged seventeen or eighteen, who was crushed by his own millstone. His shade has been seen within the red structure, where he scares people away from the hazardous machinery for their own good. His identity remains a mystery, however, one of hundreds of youths killed in workplace accidents in the days before child labor laws were enacted.

RoseMary reports that an unexplained light appears in one of the floor-to-ceiling windows of the third floor. Investigations inside find no light, but it appears again from the outside. RoseMary tells the story of a young woman, perhaps one of Bonney's daughters, Phoebe, who fell in love with a mill worker but was pushed by her lover from this window. It is not known why.

Finally, there is the story of a gruesome murder that took place inside the mill. A woman named Flo is said to have chased her philandering husband with an axe and decapitated him. A large brownish stain on the floor is supposed to be his blood. Flo and her headless husband have been reported inside the old mill. No surname for the couple exists, so this story must remain an urban legend for now.

A railroad did eventually run half a mile west of the mill grounds, but it came far too late for Edward Bonney to realize his dream of a town named for him. Although there are no records of a derailment ever occurring or of any train-related deaths on the property, people still claim to hear the haunting echo of steam engines rattling along the tracks from time to time.

5

THE HOUSE OF MANY SORROWS

I f multiple members of one family dying in the same house can cause a haunting, then the George and Elizabeth Milburn mansion in Bristol deserves to be haunted. At least three members of successive generations have died in the house, as have several subsequent residents.

George Milburn was born on May 18, 1838, in Smith Falls, Ontario, Canada. He was the nephew of George Milburn (1820–1883), founder of the Milburn Wagon Company, maker of the Milburn Electric Car that belonged to Elkhart's Nellie Knickerbocker and is now in the collection of Ruthmere Museum. The younger George's daughter, Ann, would eventually marry Clement Studebaker, who, with his brother Henry, would found the H&C Studebaker Company of South Bend, Indiana, legendary carmakers.

The younger George developed an aptitude for horticulture at an early age and eventually turned it into a career. He relocated to Bristol, Indiana, in the early 1860s, where he set up in business as a fruit grower, eventually acquiring 170 acres in the Bristol Fruit Hills. He married his first wife, Mary Elizabeth Hanford of Bristol, in 1864, but she died only two years later at the age of twenty-two.

Four years later, he married Elizabeth P. Congdon, another Bristol native, in 1868. They had two daughters and two sons. With a burgeoning family to match his growing fortune, George built his grand mansion on Vistula Street in 1879. Comprising twenty-one rooms and over four thousand square feet, the tan-brick Italianate home welcomes travelers as they enter Bristol from the east. The house occupies a prominent location on the south side of what is now State Highway 120.

George and Elizabeth's daughter Helen, born in 1877, married William Daniels of Grand Rapids, Michigan. The couple had two children during her short life. Unfortunately, she was taken ill unexpectedly in 1899. Her family thought a change of scene might benefit her health, so she boarded a train bound for Bristol to recuperate at her parents' house. The train derailed at White Pigeon, Michigan, however, and Helen, along with her eighteen-month-old daughter, was forced to complete the journey to Bristol by carriage, a distance of thirteen miles. Common opinion is that the stress of the train crash, combined with exposure to the elements, weakened Helen's already precarious health. She made it to her parents' home on Vistula Street but expired shortly after at the age of twenty-two, the same age as her father's first wife at her death.

George continued amassing his fortune, and his talents were soon recognized by the local power circles. In 1890, he was elected county auditor for one term, serving from 1891 to 1895. In 1899, he was elected

Milburn House, where no less than seven people have died over the years.

to the newly established Elkhart County Council, serving for nine years and stepping down in 1908. He died at home on February 8, 1909. Elizabeth died at home on December 21, 1933, the third person to pass away inside the mansion's walls. The Milburns and two of their children are interred at Saint John of the Cross Episcopal Cemetery in Bristol.

After Elizabeth's death, the Milburn House became a nursing home for several years. It was during this time that rumors began circulating that the house was haunted. One of the bedrooms upstairs is reputed to harbor the spirit of a senile old woman from the nursing home days. She was kept locked in the room for her own safety. Footsteps pace and shuffle around the room at all hours of the day and night and have been heard going up and down the main stairs of the house.

The form of an elderly woman has been seen peering through the curtains of the same bedroom on many occasions, noted by neighbors in the surrounding houses as well as by pedestrians on the sidewalk outside.

The house served as the Murphy Guest House bed-and-breakfast for a number of years. Eventually, the house came into the possession of Loren Arnold Congdon, no relation to Elizabeth Congdon Milburn, even though both were born in Bristol. Her family hailed from Upstate New York, while his came from Michigan. His son Earl owned the house from 1974 to 1986.

Rumors spread for many years that Loren, born in 1899, committed suicide by jumping from an east-side window in the Milburn House. His obituary, however, states that he died peacefully in a nursing home in Goshen in 1981 at the ripe old age of eighty-two. It is true that Loren had been wan for most of his life, but he still managed to outlive eight decades.

Earl Congdon sold the house to the Chaffee family in the 1980s, and they in turn sold it to Jim and Nancy Clements in the early 1990s. They set about restoring the house to its former glory. Nancy also operated a curio shop in the house called the Sugar and Spice Boutique. By the year 2000, they had sold the house to the Mihojevich family, whose children are the current owners.

Nancy Van Patten Clements Blough and her fourth husband, Steve, now live in a haunted lakeside house in Shipshewana in neighboring LaGrange County. Amid her massive collection of musical instruments (Nancy plays forty-two, "some better than others") and stained-glass lamps, Nancy recounted her experiences in the Milburn House with her husband at the time, Jim. RoseMary McDaniel and Penny Hayes were also present during the recorded interview. Unfortunately, Nancy, now approaching ninety, was unusually soft-spoken. The normally quite sensitive digital recorder picked up only faint whispers. The good news is that RoseMary and Penny are both familiar with Nancy's story and were able to fill in the details the recorder missed.

"When Nancy Blough [Clements at the time] had the home," RoseMary says, "one day she came in and—the table had been all set with the place settings and everything—and, when she came back, the tablecloth was in a pile on the chair and all the place settings and everything were perfectly in place."

Nancy, during the original interview, talked about this. She explained that the tablecloth was made by her grandmother, who asked all the family members at the time to sign their names on it. She then embroidered over their signatures, embossing them in linen for posterity. Nancy has since passed the tablecloth on to her own daughter.

Jim and Nancy claimed there were at least seven ghosts in the house. How they determined this is unknown. According to Nancy, they referred to them collectively as "George," although Helen Daniels and Loren Congdon also died in the house.

Could it be Nancy's grandmother protecting her cherished tablecloth? Perhaps. Some of the incidents that have occurred in the mansion on Vistula Street, however, hardly seem like the handiwork of a nurturing grandma. Penny says: "They had guests, and they were at the dining table. One of the guys got up to leave, and his shoelaces were tied together!"

Water in the upstairs bathroom would frequently turn ice cold or shut off altogether while Nancy was in the shower. Initially, she blamed Jim for these antics, but he continually denied involvement. Toilets also flushed spontaneously. A bar of soap bizarrely appeared in a toilet bowl one time.

In true haunted house fashion, the old push-button light switches turn on and off of their own accord. Knocks, creaks and thumps are heard at random times from different parts of the house. Doors often lock themselves from the inside. The front door, which has a bolt extending into the floor, has been found wide open from time to time.

The back stairway has a peculiar attitude, as well. "At times, you could not get into the servants' rooms," Penny Hayes explains. "The doors…you could not get in. And then, the next time, you could just walk right in."

Penny also recalls how Nancy smelled cigar smoke in the old library when nobody in the house was smoking. "There were books taken off the shelf." One book, the collected works of Mark Twain, vanished and has never been found. It is possible for old woodwork to retain odors, such as that of cigar smoke, and release them when the temperature warms up and the porous wood expands. This may account for the smell but certainly not for the moving books.

The Clementses owned a piano for many years. It wasn't until after they sold it that they began hearing piano music in the house. At first, Jim was skeptical of Nancy's claims regarding not only the plumbing but of everything else, too. He began changing his mind, however, when he and Nancy both felt unseen hands poking and nudging them.

In the room once occupied by the old woman was a corner shelf mounted several feet off the floor. On multiple occasions, Nancy found the shelf resting on the floor several feet away from the walls, its knickknacks scattered about but never broken.

The last straw, at least for a while, came one winter day when Nancy was working in the kitchen. Suddenly, she heard a banging noise and turned to see her collection of teaspoons, rack and all, fly off the wall and clatter to the floor. At that point, Nancy declared, "You won this time." She and Jim vacated the house for a while but eventually found their way back.

Nancy admits that she felt scared when they first took ownership of the Milburn mansion. The unexpected goings-on of unseen people were unnerving, but she eventually came to accept their presence.

When Jim died in 2000, the fourth person to die in the house, Nancy sold up. She eventually remarried and moved to her current home in Shipshewana. Strangely enough, the most recent residents of the house, Steve and Pauline Mihojevich, both passed away in the home in a short span of time between 2020 and 2021. The house is now owned by their children, who do not live there.

Penny Hayes sums up the history of the house—and perhaps of all haunted houses—when she says: "It's a different kind of history, but it *is* history. History of the house that people...well, a lot of people would not want to know."

6

NOT TO HIS TASTE

"Everyone is entitled to my opinion." So goes the famous quote by beloved TV newsman David Brinkley. That's not to say you're not entitled to your own opinion, just that my way is obviously better, right? That sentiment can apply to just about anything, from politics to the weather, from Beethoven to Black Sabbath. Certainly a man as upstanding as Solomon Fowler is entitled to a generous degree of respect. But does that give him the right to judge others?

Of course, we can't be certain that he is doing any such thing. But it's a possibility.

Solomon Fowler was born in Carmel, New York, on July 5, 1809, the son of Elijah and Susannah Burritt Adams Fowler. Along with his younger brother, Samuel, he was raised in a farming household to stalwart Episcopalian parents who knew the value of hard work, a value they instilled in their older son. After working on the family farm as a youth, Fowler struck out for New York City, where he worked in the offices of an oil company before moving to Indiana in 1836. Accompanying him on this new venture was his longtime friend Henry Coffin, the nephew of his boss in the oil business.

That same year, he married his first wife, Jane, born in 1812. The marriage produced no children but was a happy union. They remained married until her death on March 2, 1863. After two years alone, Fowler wed widow Martha A. Stevenson Clark (1831–1904) on Christmas Day 1865. Martha had one daughter, Cordelia, from a previous marriage.

Arriving in Bristol, Fowler and Coffin set about building a business empire together, focusing on general merchandising. Over time, the partnership dissolved, and Fowler found himself in business with A.K. Kline and William Probasco. As their mercantile grew, Fowler began to diversify his interests, becoming a senior partner in a milling concern. Steam mills, flour mills and sawmills, all owned by Fowler and associates, began popping up along the St. Joseph River. Fowler even owned a five-story furniture store in town.

The milling industry proved to be very fruitful for more than just Solomon Fowler. Competition increased to the point of violence. One evening (the date is not recorded), the Bristol Hydraulic Company, of which Fowler was president, went up in flames. Multiple buildings were consumed in the fire, which is largely believed to have been arson committed by a rival miller by the name of Boyer. However, the allegation was never proved.

Solomon and Martha built their dream home on West Vistula Street, a grand Italianate mansion overlooking Bristol's main thoroughfare, in 1868. One of the largest homes in town, it comprised more than 6,300 square feet and was situated directly opposite the millworks. They both lived in the house for the rest of their respective lives and are buried in Saint John of the Cross Episcopal Cemetery in Bristol.

Throughout his life, Solomon Fowler was regarded as an upright citizen with an impeccable reputation for honesty and integrity. He was a Mason and was buried with full Masonic honors after his death on June 19, 1877.

After Martha's death in 1904, her daughter, Cordelia Clark Sudborough, and her husband, Fred, lived in the grand mansion until their deaths. Cordelia died in 1943. They are both buried in Oak Ridge Cemetery in Bristol.

One interesting feature of the Fowler Mansion is the presence in the front yard of several gravestones, including one for a Cordelia Wheeler, a relative of Martha Fowler and possibly the namesake of Cordelia Sudborough. For many years, Wheeler's stone served as a bench in the mansion's courtyard. It now leans against the front gate, along with a couple of others, all badly weathered. Though there is no proof, the story goes that these stones were among those moved from the old Illinois Street Cemetery a few blocks away. (See chapter 9, "The House by the Town Burying Ground," for more details.)

Stuart Gardner (1916–1985) bought the house in the 1940s and is credited with installing the reflecting pool on the mansion grounds. Gardner, an inventor, created the first class-A motor home in the early 1960s, helping to cement Elkhart County's reputation as the RV capital of the world. Indeed,

Solomon Fowler Mansion, haunted by a hater of rock 'n' roll music.

most major recreational vehicle companies in America are located in Elkhart County. He sold the house to the Boger family in 1962, and their daughter Susie Peters purchased it from her folks in 1972.

Peters owned the mansion for thirty years, selling it in 2002. She was the first to note paranormal activity in the house. "I felt a great energy in my home," she says via Facebook. She recalls a recurring vision: "As I was heading up to bed several nights, I did see shadows going from one bedroom to the other on the north side of the house." She does not speculate who these shadows may have been, or even if they were male or female.

She also recalls an incident that occurred to her brother many years ago. "My brother was staying home by himself, missing our family vacation up north because of asthma, and he decided to go to the local drive-in for food. He locked the door, left, ate, returned later to find all his album covers slashed that he had been listening to. The Doors, Buffalo Springfield, etc., and all the faces had been painted blue. It certainly was a weird occurrence. He still has the albums, I believe."

Could Solomon Fowler, upright and stalwart in his public persona, have been an early hater of rock 'n' roll? Could he have objected to the radical

Brick-arched basement, Solomon Fowler Mansion, where owners have felt a presence.

sounds of The Doors and The Buffalo Springfield in *his* house? Although he died eighty years before the advent of rock music, his personality when alive suggests that he would not have been a fan. It is complete speculation, of course, but Susie Peters has no idea who else might be haunting the house.

In the same Facebook message, Peters recalls a story about the mansion. "Rumor has it there was an old woman sitting up in the north side window as people drove by on 120 [Vistula Street] and witnessed her. It used to be an old nursing home, from what I have been told, so all these spirits would make sense."

You may recall from the previous chapter that the Milburn House, located just a few blocks east on Vistula Street, was also a nursing home, and that it, too, is supposedly haunted by the ghost of an old woman, who looks out the window to the street below. It is possible that Susan Peters is mistaking the two houses, which are very much alike in appearance and contemporary with each other. Or it could be that these two houses had more in common than is obvious.

Regardless of what may have happened in the house in the past, Peters believes she was meant to own it. "When I bought 1105 from my father, I believed in my heart the home was happy to have me there and have my children (6) playing once again on the same grounds that I truly loved."

Susie Peters sold the house to Lynette and Dave Johnson in 2002. According to RoseMary McDaniel, who acted as a go-between, Lynette Johnson claims to have experienced nothing in the house in the years she lived there.

The current owner, Ana Hreniak*, does not agree. She recently hosted a paranormal investigation at the mansion that revealed some remarkable evidence. Her husband, Viktor*, spoke of feeling uncomfortable in the basement. Indeed, the brick passage, lined with arched doorways leading to a warren of interconnected rooms—including an indoor cistern that ingeniously filters out sediment—certainly has a tangible quality to its atmosphere. Regrettably, after several aborted meetings, Ana has opted not to tell her tale. Until she does, the identity of the ghost of the Fowler Mansion might forever remain unknown.

7
WHERE HISTORY LIVES ON

High school can be one of the most traumatic times in a person's life. It is a time when one's identity is shaped, for better or worse, by the times they live in, the people who surround them and the things they choose to do—or are made to do—with their lives. Budding sexuality, peer pressure and the stress of deciding who you will be for the next seventy years or so can put an enormous emotional strain on a person ill equipped at that age to deal with it all. And yet, we must.

No wonder so many schools around the world, and not just high schools, boast of having a ghost or two. Most of these fall into the category of urban legend—"This girl in my school…," "I once heard…," "This happened to a friend of mine…." Only a handful can be backed up with solid evidence. Quite often, there is a basis in fact for these events, but they are usually distorted and added on to by successive classes until the real story is beyond recognition. Still, those who make these claims often swear on a stack of yearbooks that they are telling the absolute truth.

The Washington Township High School, also known as Bristol High School and the current home of the Elkhart County Historical Society, is no exception. The original structure—square, solid, built of red brick in a Colonial Revival style—was constructed between 1903 and 1904 and originally consisted of eight rooms on two floors over a raised basement. Additions were made to the main block in 1922 and 1949. The gymnasium/auditorium was attached to the east end of the structure in 1925. The use

Washington Township High School, exterior, haunted by ethereal organ music.

of red brick for all parts of the building gives it a comfortable sense of unity today.

The last class graduated in 1966. The following year, the city put the school up for auction. Howard Rush bid successfully and donated the building and grounds to the Elkhart County Parks Department, to be used as a history museum. The museum was opened to the public in 1969 and houses more than thirty thousand items. It also hosts regular talks and programs, both in-house and off-campus.

There are at least two ghost stories attached to the old high school: that of organ music being played inside long after any such instrument resided within; and that of an unknown basketball player still dribbling away in the gym.

Penny Hayes and RoseMary McDaniel believe they know who is responsible for the ethereal music: A man who devoted his life to school, church and Calliope, the Greek muse of music.

If anyone deserves the right to a peaceful afterlife, it is Merrill "Tommy" Thompson. Whether or not he got it is a matter of conjecture. Born in Whiteland, Indiana, on November 19, 1902, Thompson exemplified the

Hoosier spirit, stretching his life over more than a century. He died in Bristol on February 20, 2004, at the incredible age of 101.

After getting his degree in education, Thompson worked briefly in Indianapolis before landing a teaching job at the Washington Township High School in 1929. Having never heard of Bristol, Indiana, he hesitated before electing to make the big move.

In the mid-1930s, he joined the Masons and eventually the Eastern Star. His future wife, Grace, was also a member of the Eastern Star. Thompson got his start playing the organ for its meetings.

Tommy Thompson was a celebrated teacher of biology and social studies at Bristol High School and is memorialized by a stone in the neighboring park. Initially, he earned $1,400 a year before the Depression hit. Having lost his job in Bristol, he returned to Indianapolis on the meager savings he'd accumulated and resumed his former work at the Wm. H. Block Co. department store, founded in 1896. After a few months of indecision, he opted to head back to Bristol with an assurance from his Block manager that he could always return if things didn't work out after a couple of years.

Back in Bristol, he taught a local girl named Grace Mosier, whose family had emigrated from Canada some years before. Her Episcopalian upbringing would eventually influence Thompson, but not for many years. Grace graduated from high school in 1931, and they married in 1940. They raised one son, Wayne, who now lives in California.

During World War II, Thompson started attending the local Methodist church. The town had no Presbyterian church, so he adapted, somewhat reluctantly. It was Merrill Thompson who was responsible for bringing the first organ to the Methodist church, where he shared performing duties with Myron Hilbish, an ancestor of RoseMary McDaniel, on piano. Thompson began taking organ lessons with V.V. Clark at the Washington Township High School until he became proficient. Indeed, music became a lifelong passion. After twenty years, he left the Methodist church for the Episcopal church, where he again played organ for twenty years or so.

In addition to his teaching duties, Thompson served as vice principal for a number of years. He also served on the board of the Bristol library for many years, further entangling himself in the field of education. It is largely because of his dogged determination in fundraising that the tiny library grew to the fine institution it is today.

When the high school closed its doors in 1966, Thompson devoted his time to the library and the Masonic Temple, but he never lost his love of music. As the Elkhart County Historical Society took over ownership of the building, it integrated parts of the school equipment into the exhibit, including two organs and an entire classroom of original desks and furnishings. (The latter has now been transferred to the former Samuel Strong School in Elkhart.) The organs were removed from the building within the last couple of years as the museum began shifting to signage to tell its story.

According to Penny Hayes, she and several other people claim to have heard organ music coming from within the building over the years. The organs were originally displayed on the second floor toward the west end of the building. Penny recalls hearing the music while in the basement auditorium, located at the east end. That means she would have heard it from two floors and several doors and cinderblock walls away.

Via email, Penny states: "When telling this story to some old alumni of the School about the organ playing, they immediately told me that it was Mr. Thompson. He played the organ all the time there."

Whether Tommy Thompson lingers because he loved teaching and playing is anybody's guess, if indeed it is him. The historical society does not allow paranormal investigations, so the true identity of the organist may never be known.

Gymnasium/auditorium of Washington Township High School, where a basketball player continues a long-lost game.

The apparition of a young basketball player has been seen in the old gym/auditorium, still playing a game that has long since ended. Who he is remains a mystery. Perhaps he is reliving that triumphant winning moment or that heartbreaking loss that ended his chances at a career. It is safe to say that no professional basketball players ever emerged from Bristol, Indiana. His legacy may go untold for eternity.

I am indebted to the Elkhart County Historical Society for much of the historical details in this book. On the subject of ghosts, though, they were reluctant—and, in one case, downright hostile—to discuss the subject. One person even went so far as to proclaim, "We don't keep track of *that* kind of history." This statement is false, however. They do have a folder in their archives containing newspaper clippings of ghost stories throughout the county. As another volunteer, Robyn Sadler*, says: "This is folklore, which is part of local history. I've never heard those stories before, but now I have." Whether she believes them or not is up to her.

It is interesting to see how different people working in the same field can have opposing viewpoints. Agreed, ghost stories are not usually quantifiable history with relics left behind, though there are some alleged spirit artifacts out there. But we may also accept that folklore truly is part of our shared culture and should be collected and preserved, if for no other reason than to remind future generations what we in the twenty-first century believe.

8
NOISES OFF

BRISTOL OPERA HOUSE, BRISTOL

D evotion to duty is an admirable quality, but it can be taken too far. What could cause someone to hang around in a theater where they never performed? While most people in the world of live theater probably dream of making a career onstage, there must be a few who are contented to work behind the curtain to ensure that everyone else looks good.

Such might be the case at the Bristol Opera House in Bristol, the current home of the Elkhart Civic Theatre. Constructed in 1896, the opera house was the dream come true for Cyrus Fulton Mosier, born on June 21, 1840, in the little upstate town of Rush, New York. His early years are obscured by time, but he had relocated to Elkhart County by 1860.

Mosier enlisted in the military in 1861, fighting first for the 12th Regiment, Indiana Infantry. After a year, he transferred to the 118th Indiana, rising to the rank of first lieutenant by the end of the war. He was discharged in 1865.

Two years prior, Mosier married Drusilla L. Rae of Orangeville, Indiana, on May 25, 1863. (Some records, including their daughter's marriage certificate, list her name as Drucilla L. Roe.) After settling in Bristol, Mosier founded the *Bristol Banner* newspaper in 1877. He also served as a state legislator in the 1860s.

Cyrus and Drusilla had two sons, Jules and Horace. No online records exist for Jules beyond the mention of his name in Cyrus's obituary from the *Goshen Democrat* of May 1, 1901. Horace, born on January 13, 1872, would grow up to follow in his father's footsteps, at least as far as editing the *Banner*, a post he would hold until the newspaper folded in 1919.

In 1896, father and son partnered in constructing a center of culture for Bristol. The iconic blue building gracing Vistula Street today was opened to the public in 1897 with a production of Gilbert and Sullivan's masterpiece, *H.M.S. Pinafore*. Unfortunately, Bristol was too small a venue to attract major stars, and the opera house hosted mostly itinerant acts willing to work for small wages. In an attempt to garner more money, the Mosiers raised the ticket price to twenty-five cents, but this proved too dear for the locals. Traveling medicine shows were very much in vogue in the late nineteenth and early twentieth centuries and were easier to book. Cyrus Mosier used his position as editor of the *Banner* to promote the opera house and its productions. His advertising stressed the gentility of his theater and the acts that performed within, proclaiming them particularly suitable for women and children.

Just as tragedy seems to follow many in show business, Horace Mosier was no exception. He married his first wife, Jennie E. Bickel, in 1892. The marriage produced no offspring, and Jennie died, still a young woman, at the age of thirty-five. After a decent interval, Horace wed Inez Klosz of Plattsville, Ontario, Canada, in 1911. Inez gave birth to a child in December

Bristol Opera House, Bristol's most haunted location.

1923, a daughter they christened Geraldine Louise. Sadly, Geraldine passed away in February 1924, only two months old.

Cyrus Mosier passed away on April 26, 1901, a mere sixty years old, leaving Horace as sole proprietor and operator. Drusilla Mosier departed this earth in 1930, aged eighty-five.

Over time, live shows at the opera house became increasingly unproductive, and the theater was all but abandoned by 1915. In an attempt to keep things afloat, Horace converted the venue into a cinema, catering to the new sensation of silent movies. Tickets were a dime for a Saturday or Sunday showing. In 1917, he remodeled the interior to entice new business. This new business model ultimately proved fruitless, as the rise in automobiles made it easier for people to drive to Elkhart, or even South Bend, to enjoy more sophisticated entertainment in more luxurious surroundings.

In the following decades, the Bristol Opera House ceased to host theatrical entertainment of any form. The building was put to various uses, including as a roller-skating rink, a basketball court and a meetinghouse. By 1940, the building was in an advanced state of decay, suitable only for storage space.

Horace Mosier died on October 7, 1956, and was buried with the rest of his family at Saint John of the Cross Episcopal Cemetery in Bristol.

The year 1960 proved to be a turning point for the wood-frame structure on Vistula Street. Slated for demolition, it was reprieved at the last minute by the Elkhart Civic Theatre, undaunted by the massive renovations required to make the opera house habitable again. Through vigorous campaigning and fundraising, the organization amassed $5,000 with which to begin work. The new owners set about modernizing the building while doing their best to maintain its historic appearance. The original chandelier was refurbished by contributions from the Bristol fire chief and the employees of the Bristol Band Instrument Company. The rejuvenated facility was reopened to the public in July 1961 and continues to host live theater and other events today.

While the current staff is no doubt devoted to the old place, no one can make that claim more fervently than Percival Peter Hilbert, who worked as a handyman for many years. "Percy," as he is known to the current crew, was born in Louisville, Kentucky, on February 13, 1875. Along with his first wife, Elizabeth Tait Hilbert, he raised three children, Emrie Withrow, Mary Elizabeth and Roberta Alice. After his first wife's death, he married Martha Myrtle Roberts. Percy passed away on August 5, 1956, and is buried, along with Elizabeth, in Chapel Hill Memorial Gardens in Osceola, Indiana.

It is said that Percy and his family, after losing their home in a fire, lived in the Bristol Opera House for some time. There exist no records to substantiate this claim. However, current staff members credit Percy as the most prominent of the ghosts said to haunt the old theater. Described as a prankster, he is said to hang around the ladies' dressing rooms, presumably trying to catch a peek. He has also been spotted in the right-hand aisle of the theater.

Staff and actors alike claim that Percy likes to brush up against them, even grabbing actors' costumes and yanking them back as they attempt to make their entrance onto the stage. He has a particular aversion to musicals, and his antics tend to increase during their production.

Two female ghosts also inhabit the venerable structure overlooking downtown Bristol. A little girl dubbed "Beth" peers out from behind the curtain at stage left, checking on the audience, perhaps to ensure that they are having a good time. A middle-aged woman the staff refers to as "Helen" has a particular fondness for directors and producers, making certain they come to no harm.

How any of these people met their deaths is unrecorded, as is the connection Beth and Helen have to the old theater. Whatever the case may be, they have endowed the Bristol Opera House with the reputation of being the most haunted building in Bristol, if not in all of Elkhart County.

9

THE HOUSE BY THE
TOWN BURYING GROUND

Every now and then, you come across a tale that sounds as if it came straight from the pages of a Hollywood script. Such is the case of the Cusimano house in downtown Bristol. Because of the sensitive nature of the story, most real names, as well as the photo and exact address of this house, are being omitted.

In 1982, Warner Studios released *Poltergeist*, a now-classic horror film starring Craig T. Nelson and JoBeth Williams. Spoiler alert: The film tells the story of a young family that buys a house that turns out to be built on an old cemetery from which only the headstones have been removed. The bodies were left in place and a subdivision built on top of them. The deception was not revealed until too late. Lest we think this is just fiction, it is not. The movie, highly stylized, was based on the true story of a housing development in the Houston suburb of Crosby, Texas, built on a nineteenth-century graveyard known as Black Hope Cemetery. Books and TV shows, independent of each other, exist to document the shameful truth of this story.

Black Hope is not the only cemetery to be defiled in this manner. The Illinois Cemetery in Bristol, Indiana, suffered the same fate in 1917. Also known as the Town Burying Ground, this cemetery, covering a portion of land at the corner of Illinois and Depot Streets, is officially no more. The gravestones were moved to Oak Ridge Cemetery to make room for houses. The corpses, however, were left in situ, the houses built on top of them. In all, the cemetery ground, small to begin with, was divided into four lots. Oddly enough, the Cusimano house was not built on one of these.

The Cusimano house sits adjacent to the original cemetery, though its driveway passes through the former grounds. An attractive home covered in black shakes with white trim, tucked away from prying eyes behind other houses and a stand of trees, this small house, built in 1860, is currently the home of Crystal Cusimano*. Although Crystal does not claim to hear or see anything untoward in the house, her best friend of twenty-plus years, Jynnifer Woodfield*, has claimed a number of experiences while visiting the house.

Jynnifer, a social worker trained to be both observant and compassionate, recounts several incidents at the house on Illinois Street. Via Facebook, she tells the following stories:

> In September of 2020, I spent the night at Crystal's home. I was living in Indianapolis at the time, so when I would come visit, I would just stay in her spare bedroom. Earlier that evening I had gone in the basement with Crystal to get some supplies for a party we were throwing for our friends. I had never been in her basement before. While in the basement, I asked Crystal if she had ever noticed any weird vibes down there. She said no, but she's not very sensitive to that stuff and she actually doesn't believe in spirits or ghosts. She did say that she had heard rumors that her home was part of the Underground Railroad, so I just assumed it was some anxious, residual energy from that. We went upstairs and decorated for the party and went to bed around midnight.
>
> That night I had a weird dream about a sweet old lady who had passed away. I was at her funeral in the dream. We appeared to be at the Methodist Church in Bristol, and there were blue flowers everywhere. I didn't think much of it at the time because I have weird dreams a lot. I was telling Crystal about it and she said maybe my dream had been about Lillian Carey*, one of the previous home owners. Crystal later found out that Lillian did have blue flowers at her funeral. I then went back to Crystal's house around February 2021. We went in her basement again and I was able to confirm that Lillian was the lady in the basement.

Jynnifer has had other encounters with the paranormal in other locations. Her mother's house, located on Division Street in Bristol, is haunted by the ghost of an unidentified but benevolent man. When Jynnifer, who claims to have psychic abilities and does house readings and cleansings, visited this house to do a reading, she detected the presence of two men, one good, one malevolent. She was able to banish the negative spirit while leaving the good one to get on with his haunting. Whether she should have helped him cross over as well is a matter of opinion. Perhaps he wasn't ready to let go.

The most bizarre incident occurred a couple of days after the aforementioned party, when Jynnifer was back home in Indianapolis.

I almost always bring my Celestite stone and other crystals with me when I go to places outside of my normal living space so I don't bring home any spiritual hitchhikers. But I happened to forget it this time. Later that Sunday, when I got back to my house, I was laying [sic] in bed and everyone was sleeping, so I was the only one awake. I noticed a small blonde boy in my bedroom doorway. He communicated that he was lost and wanted to find his mom. My house did have a spirit residing there and I had some issues with it in the past, so I wasn't that surprised that someone else had shown up.

After about two weeks of doing some channeling with the little boy, I found out his name started with an "M" and he had passed away at about three years old from something to do with his stomach. He didn't know his name or why he followed me from Crystal's house. I just figured he followed me because I'm a mom and I have two boys not that much older than he was. And he said that he stayed in the basement at Crystal's, and he liked the old lady that was there too.

Eventually, Jynnifer was able to track down the boy's parents and cross him over to reunite the family.

Then around July of 2021, I was telling my mom about the little boy who had been in Crystal's basement and she turned as white as a ghost and asked if I had seen Marty Schiffer*. My mom said that Marty had passed away at about three years old from what they thought was some kind of stomach issue. Turns out Marty was the son of Joni Schiffer*, who was a good friend of both me and Crystal and she had passed away in 2008 or 2009 (I can't remember the exact year). And Crystal also has some of Joni's personal items in her house. So Marty could have followed me because he knew I was connected to his mom. But he could have also just followed me home since he knew I'm able to communicate with him. But the connection was pretty interesting.

RoseMary McDaniel provided a copy of Marty's obituary, confirming that he died at the age of two of a congenital defect of the diaphragm in 1983. He was buried in Oak Ridge Cemetery in Bristol. Further research revealed that Marty lived in the house immediately next to Crystal's, one of the houses on the original Town Burying Ground. Obviously, having died in 1983, Marty had not been one of the unfortunates left to be built over. Still, it does explain his attachment to Jynnifer. Perhaps sensing she was psychic, Marty figured she would be a likely source to reunite him with his mother.

Children play a large part in Jynnifer's psychic history. She had a sister, Ronnie*, who died as a child in 1990 and is buried in Oak Ridge Cemetery. One day, Jynnifer took her own young daughter to the cemetery but did not tell her whose grave they were visiting. She figured it would be too traumatizing for her little girl to know that children her own age could die. Thus, having not told her daughter, Jynnifer was startled when her daughter spontaneously called out, "Hi, Ronnie!"

The house on Illinois Street, built in 1860, is still haunted by the ghost of Lillian Carey, even though Lillian, too, was alive long after the disgrace that befell the old Illinois Cemetery, having died in 2002. What's peculiar is that Lillian's headstone does not give a death date, only a birth year, 1930. Penny Hayes provided pictures of Lillian's and Marty's headstones, but she did confirm that Lillian is, in fact, deceased. Why the omission on Lillian's stone? Maybe this was Lillian's way of ensuring she'd live forever. Her memory, at least, is doing a good job!

If there are other spirits dwelling in the Cusimano house or any of the four houses built on the actual burial grounds—one of which has been vacant for years, another of which burned down and was replaced early in the twenty-first century—Jynnifer has not said. Perhaps she has not read these houses. Perhaps their owners would rather not know.

10

THE PAST IS PRESENT

One popular theory behind haunting involves home renovation or redecorating, the theory being that spirits in a house find the changes disruptive or, worse, a shocking violation of *their* home. Such chaos often stirs up paranormal activity in otherwise quiet locales.

That may be the case with the Simonton House at the corner of Cassopolis and Floyd Streets in Elkhart. Owners Carol and Jim Reeves renovated inside and out this beautiful, brown-brick, black-trim Italianate home. Carol has filled the house with gorgeous Victorian furniture. The rooms are bejeweled with stained-glass lamps and windows. The woodwork throughout glows with renewed vigor, reflecting the love and attention to detail the couple has put into their historic home. They did not live in the home during the bulk of the renovations, so they cannot attribute the ghostly goings-on to their handiwork. However, the possibility remains.

Built in 1890 for David S. Simonton, the gorgeous house sits on a large, grassy lot overlooking the busy thoroughfare of Cassopolis Street, just a few blocks north of the Wilson Wilbert Wilt House (see chapter 11). David was born to Samuel and Anna Pierce Simonton on December 16, 1817, in Clark County, Ohio. At the age of thirty-two, he, along with his family, relocated to Elkhart. In his early manhood, according to a death notice in the *Fort Wayne Sentinel*, David worked as a contractor, building many homes in the Elkhart area and acquiring substantial tracts of land in the northern part of town, including the lot on which his house still stands.

Simonton House, where a prankster still roams.

On January 22, 1844, David Simonton married Emily Allen of Owasco, New York. According to Findagrave.com, they raised two daughters, Emma and Clara, in Elkhart, although the obituary in the Fort Wayne paper makes no mention of them. It does state that David and Emily had a son. There is a Lawrence Simonton, born in 1845, buried in the family plot in Grace Lawn Cemetery, but Findagrave.com does not list his parents or any siblings. Carol and Jim are certain that Lawrence was David's son.

Emily Simonton died on March 31, 1898, and David passed a few years later, on December 29, 1901, aged eighty-four, one of the area's wealthiest citizens. Both are buried in Grace Lawn. Among the other testaments to his life are Simonton Lake up near the Michigan line and Simonton Street, which bisects northern Elkhart, just two blocks south of his home. Interestingly, David opted to build a small house for a man of such vast wherewithal. The elegant house encompasses less than 1,800 square feet.

At David's death, Lawrence Simonton inherited the house on Cassopolis. At the time, the land on the opposite side of Cassopolis Street, much of it belonging to David, was in a different township. The City of Elkhart wanted that land for itself and apparently wasn't averse to acquiring it by ruthless means. According to Jim Reeves, Lawrence "got angry with the town because they took all that land." Eventually, Lawrence sold the land to

David Simonton, the original owner.

a religious organization, which in turn sold the house to Olive O. Heisel (1898–1981) and her husband, Charles (1882–1944).

"Olive ran a bar and hotel downtown," Carol says. After her husband died, "she was staying at the hotel a lot, so RoseMary [McDaniel] thinks that Olive rented rooms here. And then Olive sold it to RoseMary and her husband, Carl. Then, when she and Carl moved to Bristol, their son moved in here."

Carl worked as a tool-and-dye machinist, operating his business out of the Simonton House. He passed away on July 18, 2013, of a sudden illness at the age of sixty-eight and is buried in Oak Ridge Cemetery in Bristol. His occupation may have a relevance to some of the incidents Carol and Jim Reeves have experienced.

Devin, RoseMary's son, died in Battle Creek, Michigan, on November 5, 2018, also after a sudden illness. He is also buried in Oak Ridge Cemetery. He was only fifty-five. During his life, Devin served his fellow man in many noble capacities. He was an environmental specialist in Cassopolis, Michigan, serving as an advocate for the disabled and the handicapped, as well as volunteering for hospice at area nursing homes. He had a penchant for electronics and local history. Earlier in his life, he owned and operated a café and bakery and ran a fifty-acre farm in Dowagiac, Michigan. Prior to that, he worked in the RV industry.

RoseMary thinks Devin may still be haunting the Simonton House, based on some of the incidents Jim and Carol have reported to her in the last few years. According to her, Devin was a bit of a prankster. Carol, at least, disagrees. She and Jim had known both Carl and Devin. "I would almost think it was not Devin, because Devin didn't seem like the playful sort to me."

Jim and Carol purchased the house from RoseMary in 2018 and set about restoring it over the next few years. Many of the incidents they describe focus on tools. One afternoon, Jim was working upstairs when his hammer mysteriously vanished. A few days later, Carol was coming down the stairs and found the hammer on top of a large cabinet that sits near the foot of the stairs.

Additionally, Jim says, "There was some toolboxes that belonged to RoseMary's husband in the basement, and the keys were in 'em, 'cause I'd just went through 'em. So I carried 'em up the stairs, got 'em out to the garage, and opened 'em back up and the keys had gone. So I came back in, thinking somehow they fell out, even though everything was completely closed. I've never been able to find 'em."

The fact that Carl McDaniel had been a machinist suggests that he may be the ghost-in-residence and was, perhaps, displeased with Jim handling *his* tools. People who make a living with tools are often fastidious with them, sometimes to the point of obsession. Perhaps Carl was trying to tell Jim to leave things the way he found them.

Doors play a recurring role in Jim's and Carol's experiences, as well. One night around midnight, Carol was outside, taking their dog Baxter for a walk. Returning to the back door, she heard the deadbolt (an electronic one requiring the push of a button to lock it) click into place. "I did get a chill. It did scare me when that deadbolt went off 'cause I thought, 'Do you not want me in here?'" She laughs about it now, but at the time, "That was the only time I felt odd. That was freaky. Very, very freaky."

Carol also talks about seeing a figure move swiftly past the bedroom door upstairs. Naturally thinking it was Jim, she was startled to discover he was nowhere near.

While preparing dinner one night, Carol heard a pantry door open behind her. She turned to watch the door swing completely open until it was resting against the wall. The door is held closed by a magnetic catch with a pretty strong pull, and the door itself is well balanced. Gravity does not cause it to swing freely in either direction.

The Reeveses also tell of a recurring incident in their living room. Their sofa faces a flat-screen TV hanging on the wall. Just to the right of the TV is a pair of French doors leading into the hallway. From where they sit, the doors are clearly visible. From time to time, they will look away from the

French doors, Simonton House, that open and close by themselves.

TV to discover that the doors, previously opened, are suddenly closed, or vice versa. The doors themselves make no sound on these occasions, but the movement should have been quite clear to Carol and Jim in their peripheral vision. However, neither has seen the doors move of their own volition.

Incidentally, the threshold of this door was, until Carol and Jim floored over it, marred by a large, bloodlike stain they could never remove. Whether it is blood remains unanswered. It may be a chemical that Carl used on his machines in the basement. Without proper chemical analysis, this question will probably remain unanswered. RoseMary has no explanation, either.

The ghost, whoever it may be, has a penchant for picking Carol's most vulnerable moments to strike. "I was taking a bath one night, and the door was closed. Jim was down here, watching TV, and I distinctly heard three knocks on the door. I said, 'Yeah? Come in.' And nothing. So, when I got my jammies on, I said [to Jim], 'What did you want?' He said, 'I never left the couch.'"

About a month before our interview, Carol was taking a hot, steamy shower. She moved to the opposite end of the tub to grab a bottle of shampoo. "When I came back, it was, like, ice-cold." Under normal circumstances, this may be attributed to a plumbing issue, but how could the water go from one extreme to the other in the time it takes to step a few feet and grab a shampoo bottle? She gestures with her hands. "It was like this much was steamy hot, and this much was icy cold."

Jim recalls an incident that happened to Carol while they were in bed. "It felt like a hand touched her on the back."

Carol emphasizes, "Three taps, one, two, three. I think I jumped five feet because he was asleep. His back was to me. It wasn't his hand."

An incident involving TV remotes makes RoseMary believe Devin may be responsible for at least some of the goings-on in the Simonton House, given Devin's love of electronics. Gesturing to the coffee table in front of him, Jim explains: "Our TV remote we would keep on this table right here. When I came downstairs one morning, the remote to the TV was *gone!*" He says this word with particular emphasis. "We turned this house upside-down lookin' for that remote. Nowhere to be found. So we went out and bought a universal one and put it there, and it wasn't much longer that one disappeared." Two or three weeks, Carol says. "And then the old one was back!"

Carol adds, "We never found the universal one."

The staircase leading to the second floor has an atmosphere that Carol in particular finds disturbing. On the wall over the lower portion of the steps, directly across from the top landing, hangs a large mirror. Carol says she never looks in that mirror as she's descending the steps for fear of what she might see behind her. She also describes the constant feeling that something wants to push her down the stairs.

Jim recounts an incident involving the stairs. "When my sister and brother-in-law came, he stood at the bottom of these stairs and said there's an energy at those stairs. He couldn't place it, but he could feel it." Their little dog refused to climb the stairs and had to be carried up to the guest room.

Carol and Jim's dog Baxter has also sensed an occasional presence in the dining room. At times, he will trot happily across the polished hardwood floor without so much as a pause, while at other times, he refuses point-blank to enter the room. He behaved perfectly normally throughout our interview, crossing the room more than once without hesitating.

Baxter has been acquitted of another peculiar incident, which happened to Jim in the garage. "The big garage door—I was workin' out there one day and I went to shut it. It got almost all the way down and then, all of a sudden, it ticked back off again to open up. I thought maybe it was Baxter, 'cause Baxter was in the truck at the time. I thought maybe the remote's in the truck and he's hittin' the button. So I went to look and the remote wasn't in there. I came back in and the remote was layin' on my toolbox. And that went on probably four or five times. I had to actually unplug the opener to get it to stop."

Shades of Devin McDaniel's love of electronic gadgetry again? Could this also explain how Carol became locked out of the house?

One final incident, recurring, involves a picture frame. At the time of our interview, the frame was empty and resting on top of the same cabinet where the hammer mysteriously appeared. Carol explains that the picture that occupied the frame had the annoying habit of falling out of the frame and slipping behind the cabinet, even when held in place by layers of duct tape. The house is decorated with a number of photos from Elkhart's history. Although the Reeveses did not mention what this particular picture shows, one has to wonder if it is something a previous resident does not wish to recall.

With the exception of Carol's temporary banishment from the house, she and Jim have never been truly ill at ease in the house, certainly not to the point of being driven out.

"Everything that's happened to us here," Jim says, "we never felt afraid or threatened by it. It's just, you know, wow, that happened!"

11

"WHEN THE LAST ONE LETS YOU GO"

WILSON WILBERT WILT HOUSE, ELKHART

I believe everything happens for a purpose. Not to say that we don't have free will or that we don't make our own decisions. I fervently believe we all shape our own destinies via the choices we make, for better or worse. Sometimes, the choices are made for us by other people. The point is, I believe nothing happens for no reason. And we may not always be privy to those reasons.

You may disagree, and that is your right—your decision.

But here's a little food for thought. On the night of June 1, 2021, I was in my bedroom at the Wilson Wilbert Wilt House around midnight when I had the inspiration to write a song. So I got out my pen and notepad, which I keep nearby for this exact purpose, and scrawled out a lyric titled "When the Last One Lets You Go." It's based on the theory that a person never really dies until the last person who knew them on earth has also passed away. Only then does a person's spirit truly cease to exist on this plane. In other words, they only really die when there's no one left to remember them firsthand. I don't know why I chose to write that song. Maybe something in a song on the CD I listened to earlier that night or in the book I was reading inspired me. At any rate, I had the idea, so I wrote the song.

The next morning, when I got to work at Ruthmere Museum, I read my emails as usual. Among them was a message from my boss that Ruthmere's founding director, Robert Beardsley, had passed away in Florida on June 1 around 9:20 p.m.

Wilson Wilbert Wilt House, where a little girl makes occasional appearances.

I'm not saying Robert came to me as a ghost and asked me to write a song about him. The song is not about him. I had no idea he had passed away only a few hours earlier in a state a thousand miles away. I only met Robert once, about five years prior, so we weren't close. There's no reason his family would have contacted me to let me know he was gone. Therefore, I can say with all honesty that I did not know he was dead.

In 2020, I was given the privilege of compiling a book of essays Robert Beardsley had written for the Ruthmere newsletter over a period of seventeen years. Because of the success of this project, Robert gave me the additional charge of editing his autobiography. Needless to say, I was deeply honored with this opportunity. A person's writing, especially an autobiography, is a tangible part of that person's soul. To be given the responsibility of handling someone's life story is a sacred trust.

Therefore, it all seems too coincidental to be coincidental, if you know what I mean. In working on Robert's writings for the last two years, I feel I have come to know him very thoroughly. I was the first person, as far as I know, to read his life story. I was the one he trusted to do his words and his memories—and now his memory—the justice they so rightly deserve.

I do not consider myself psychic to any notable degree. I've had a handful of premonitions over the course of my life, all inconsequential and forgettable. And I do believe that humans as a species have innate psychic abilities built into their brains. It's just that most people never learn to develop these powers for whatever reason. Thus, I do not claim some precognition about Robert's death when I began writing "When the Last One Lets You Go." Even though Robert knew where I lived, he had no connection with the Wilt House and never visited it, as far as I know, although he did spend much of his childhood at Ruthmere and at his Uncle Hub's house, both just one block west on Beardsley Avenue.

Marcia VanZile and I have lived in this beautiful, red-brick, Colonial Revival house with soaring Doric columns on Beardsley Avenue for six years now. I can't speak for her, but I have experienced an occasional whiff of roses, coffee and other unexpected scents, particularly in my bedroom, where there are no flowers or colognes. I don't drink coffee, so I can rule that out. These scents usually manifest well into the night, long after Marcia has gone to sleep, so I know she's not making coffee at 1:00 a.m.

I took a series of photographs in our dining room a couple of years ago, right after we installed our new crystal chandelier. It is brand new, so it is highly unlikely that anything has attached itself to it. The rest of the furniture in the dining room is antique, spanning the first half of the twentieth century, so it is possible that something wedded itself emotionally to one of these pieces. At the time I took the photo, I saw or felt nothing unusual in the dining room. But when reviewing the photos, I saw something unexplainable in one of them, reproduced here. If you look at the wall below the apple painting, you can see a rounded shadow. What that may be is anybody's guess. Since the chandelier was between me and the wall, it could not have cast my shadow on the wall, so we can rule that out. Marcia wasn't home at the time, so I know it's not her shadow. The photo remains a mystery.

The image is also interesting from a ghost-hunting point of view, because it illustrates a common happening in supposedly haunted locations, an unconscious practice known as matrixing—the mind's attempt to make sense of randomness. Look at the window to the left of the picture. Can you spot a face looking in? Yes? Well, look again. If you break it down logically, you can easily conclude that this "face" is the result of the chandelier illuminating the rippled glass in the window, creating the illusion of a rather stiff face staring back at you. It can be unnerving if you don't know what you're looking for.

Dining room, Wilt House, showing mysterious shadow beneath apple painting.

There have been other occurrences in the Wilt House, many of them recent. One night shortly after writing "When the Last One Lets You Go," I was working at my computer when I heard distinct footsteps above me. The library, where I was working, is in a one-story wing, so there is no room or corridor above, just a two-foot-high space where a slanted ceiling is hidden by a drop ceiling. I think I can dismiss the possibility of a squirrel or other animal. These steps were heavy, like boots, widely spaced and distinctive. But what were they doing on the roof? I heard them again a couple of months later.

The following night, just past midnight, I was again at work on my computer when I heard a distinct, protracted whistling sound in my left ear. Marcia was already in bed, and the cats were nowhere to be found. Besides, cats don't whistle. I heard it again the following afternoon and several times since, and not always in the library.

The library door will occasionally open of its own accord while I'm in there, usually in the late evening after Marcia has gone to bed. On these occasions, the cats are conspicuously absent. Come to think of it, this is often around the time when a little girl might be getting ready for bed. The significance of this will become clear shortly.

Upstairs hallway, Wilt House, where shadow figures have been seen.

Marcia and I have both, independently, seen a shadow form moving along the upstairs hallway near the bathroom. In my case, the figure was gray and featureless, about six feet tall, standing well away from the wall. It appeared to be coming toward me as I approached the bathroom. Gone in an instant, it gave me no time to be scared, as is often the case with paranormal events.

Oddly enough, since I began working on this book, the house has become noticeably less silent—nothing frightening, merely curious. I guess I shouldn't be surprised that there might be residual energy in this house. Past occupants aside, the house is crammed with antiques in every room, a passion of mine. I even have an old bed knob from a notoriously haunted orphanage in Marquette, Michigan. If people can become emotionally attached to items during their lifetime, then why can't they continue that connection after death? Maybe someone is drawn to a chair or a piece of glass that now belongs to me.

Perhaps the spirits simply kept quiet until I began working on this book. Then, when they realized I was emotionally open (or attuned), they felt comfortable making themselves known. Either that, or this project has made me more aware of my surroundings. I won't say "paranoid," because I have absolutely no sense that they're "out to get me."

Additionally, many "suspicious" events can be traced to Duchess and Squeaky, our cats, who maraud around the house at all times of the day and night. The Squeakinator, in particular, runs on high octane twenty-four/seven and can be counted on to make a riot out of a rubber band.

The house was built in 1903 for Wilson Wilbert Wilt, a butcher (though a 1906 Elkhart city directory lists him as a dance instructor!) and the founder of Wilt's Grocery Stores, which eventually grew into Wilt's Supermarkets, a chain that stretched all the way to the Pacific Northwest, the only place they still exist. The house sits on land that used to host one of Havilah Beardsley's original mills on the St. Joseph River. It is possible that the spirits are connected to the mill in some way, but this is just a guess.

Wilt (1872–1940) married Margaret J. Diehl (1873–1951) in the first decade of the 1900s. They had one child, a daughter named Margaret after her mother.

The younger Margaret was born on April 26, 1909, but only lived to the age of twenty-seven, passing away on February 22, 1937. In that short life, however, Margaret was married twice, which is the first part of the complicated history of the house on Beardsley. She married her first husband, Harley L. Deckard, in 1928 but by 1935 had gotten remarried, to Howard Evan Rush. Neither marriage produced any children, so romantics of the world may conclude that daughter Margaret died pining for the love of a child destined not to be.

But let's back up a hair.

According to his obituary, Harley Deckard ran a grocery store in Elkhart for several years. Could this have been a Wilt's Grocery Store? Although there is no evidence of this today, it seems likely, given what was to happen in the succeeding years. After he and Margaret were divorced, Harley married Mary Louise Moore in 1944—June 6, 1944, to be precise. D-Day! It's rather amusing to contemplate that, as Harley and Mary Louise were walking down the aisle, the Allied forces were storming the beaches at Normandy. Talk about a metaphor!

At any rate, Harley and Mary Louise had several children, among them a son named Joseph, born in 1946. What makes this unusual is that after Margaret Diehl Wilt passed away in 1951, the Wilt House came into the ownership of one Joseph E. Deckard! There are no records of any other Joseph Deckard living in Elkhart. This implies that Wilson Wilt (or his wife) was very attached to ex-son-in-law Harley. Wilson died in 1940, six years before Joseph E. Deckard was born. Ownership of the house passed from Margaret Diehl Wilt to her late daughter's ex-husband's son from his second marriage! Not even a blood relative. What must Wilson have thought about that? To make things stranger, Joseph was only five years old when he inherited the house, the closest thing Margaret had to a grandson.

Joseph Deckard (1946–2009) owned the house until 1963 or '64, at which time it stumbled from one owner to the next in rapid succession—three owners in three years. The house sat vacant for a further two years before being purchased by insurance agent John C. Morgan in 1969. He lived there for more than a decade before selling to a subsequent owner. Several more owners occupied the house over the next twenty-two years, among them a car salesman and a voice teacher. From 2012 to 2016, the house was owned by David Garcia and used as a rental property before Marcia and I purchased it in April 2016. During its years as a rental, the house was occupied by only one family, who must have had a young daughter. The room that is now our library, where I keep my computer, was decorated with stickers of butterflies and fairies when we moved in. The windows of this room overlook Beardsley Avenue, which may be significant given what happened next.

No evidence has yet surfaced to suggest anyone has died in the house. However, on the evening of August 26, 2017, a horrific car accident occurred in front of the house. A man and a woman driving west on Beardsley Avenue plowed into a family of five who were walking on the sidewalk on their way home from getting ice cream. Three people died: a twenty-two-year-old man, an eleven-year-old girl and an eight-month-old infant. The other two pedestrians incurred serious injuries but survived. A commemorative sign has since been erected at the intersection.

Intersection of Beardsley Avenue and Cassopolis Street from the Wilt House porch, site of a tragic accident in 2017.

The person driving the car sped away from the crash site, hitting two more cars in the process, before disappearing into the night. Three days later, police found the car hidden beneath a tarp in a parking lot at the factory where the husband worked. The couple vanished into thin air for nearly four months before turning themselves in. The husband took the blame, although one of the survivors claimed he saw a woman driving as he clung to the hood. Both husband and wife went to prison.

Is it possible that one of the victims gravitated to our house instead of moving on? Perhaps he or she recognized it as a friendly house—may have even visited former residents (the little girl who slept in the library?)—and, in the confusion of not knowing they were dead, took refuge here. Maybe more than one spirit. The heavy footsteps I heard overhead sounded like a man in boots, while the whistle could have come from a playful little girl. Why they took nearly four years to reveal themselves is a mystery unto itself. Perhaps they've been here all along and we just didn't notice. We tend to blame the cats for a lot that happens here. As much as I love the thought of having a ghost in the house, I sincerely hope I am wrong and that these three souls managed to cross over to eternal rest. There's nothing more heartbreaking than a child lost and confused and unable to move forward.

To add to this, in recent months I have seen the figure of a little girl standing in the living room, watching through the glass door as I work on my computer in the library. Every time, I catch only a glimpse of her out of the corner of my eye, but she always appears the same: about four feet tall, brown hair to her shoulders and a pinkish-yellow dress. She could be about eleven years old. As soon as she becomes aware of *my* awareness, she disappears. I admit it could be my eyes playing tricks on me, but would they do so in exactly the same way multiple times?

Perhaps, like Robert Beardsley, she just wants to be remembered.

My point in all of this is that I have no reason to suspect that I was visited by Robert Beardsley the night he passed away. I just find it interesting and fascinating that I could have written such a poignant and timely song lyric, given that I have been entrusted with polishing Robert's life story and getting it ready to share with the world. For eternity.

You never truly die until the last person who knew you on earth is no longer living. You be the judge.

12

THE ONLY PLACE HE FELT SAFE

I s it possible to haunt a building you never even saw during your lifetime? Some people say it is. Spirits are often attached to the land on which they dwelt, and so they migrate from one building to the next on that same piece of dirt. This may explain what the current owner says is happening at the Samuel Strong School on Lexington Avenue in Elkhart.

Samuel Smith Strong was born in Cuyahoga, Ohio, on June 27, 1817, the son of Walter and Betsy Strong. Raised on a farm, Samuel knew all about the benefits of hard work. Records of his life are patchy and inconsistent, unless this enterprising man lived life as a jack-of-all-trades. According to the census records for 1860, 1870 and 1880, Strong worked as a merchant, a farmer and a hosiery manufacturer, respectively. Variety may be the spice of life, but what about death? We do know he owned a store on Main Street in 1860, but the nature of the business is not recorded. He was also involved, one would assume financially, in the construction of the first dam across the St. Joseph River in 1867–68.

Strong married twice during his lifetime. His first wife, Harriet Stillman, was born in Elkhart, where they wed. His second wife, Louisa Melissa Strong, a distant cousin from back in Cuyahoga, was the stepdaughter of a prominent Ohio judge, Erastus Miles. These two marriages begat eleven children between 1849 and 1877: Rowland, Norman, Charles, Mary, Walter, Edward, James, Frederick, Laura Bonnybell, George and Clarence.

Over the course of his working life, Samuel Strong amassed quite a fortune. The 1870 census states his net worth at $26,000, including the property he owned.

In 1884, he and Louisa built their grand mansion, a white-columned beauty on what would eventually be called Strong Avenue in Elkhart. This house would later be owned by band-instrument mogul C.G. Conn.

While there are no records of his doing so—he did not even have an obituary in any of the local newspapers—it seems likely that Strong was quite a philanthropist. Perhaps he owned the wedge-shaped parcel of land surrounded by Lexington Avenue, Third Street and Vistula Street in downtown Elkhart. Perhaps he deeded it to the city to build a school. Again, there are no records of this, so this is pure speculation. At any rate, there was a school on this triangular lot prior to 1892. Once again, newspaper accounts are conspicuously mute, hinting only at the presence of the school. No name is forthcoming.

Samuel Strong died on February 19, 1892, in Elkhart and is buried in Grace Lawn Cemetery. In that same year, the city elected to build a new high school on the Lexington Avenue lot. The brooding structure, a mass of brown limestone in the Romanesque Revival style, consisted of thirteen rooms and cost $36,000, according to a 1966 article in the *Elkhart Truth*. Originally, the small point of land at the western apex of the triangle (between Lexington and Vistula) was intended to be a city park, but Elkhart never exercised its option, and the land instead became a playground for the school.

The Lexington Avenue school served as the town high school until 1912, when the student body was relocated to the new high school on Franklin Street, itself torn down many years ago to make room for the Elkhart City Court House (now, in turn, facing possible demolition as of this writing). With the departure of the high school, the building on Lexington was remodeled and turned into an elementary school. It was at this juncture that the building officially became the Samuel Strong School.

In 1915, according to city statistics, Strong had a student population of 333, which had grown to 439 by 1918, along with twelve teachers, making it the third-biggest school in Elkhart.

The 1966 *Truth* article chronicles the life of Emily Darling Schafer (1874–1966), the first female principal at Strong School, a position she held until her retirement in 1942. Schafer organized the county's first Parent-Teacher Organization. She eventually moved to California, where she passed away.

Samuel Strong School continued serving the community until declining enrollment brought an end to its days as a place of learning in 1975. The

Samuel Strong School, now a dentist's office, where children continue to play.

building sat empty for a short while before being purchased by Dr. Darren Austin*, DDS. Austin renovated the interior once more, converting the building into his dental office, a purpose the building still serves today.

Although he claims to be a skeptic, Austin reports a number of incidents in the old stone building on Lexington. Looking at the building from outside, it's not hard to imagine. The building is three stories tall, and its gloomy exterior—replete with boarded-up windows around the entire top floor—belies the warm, even charming, interior that greets patients today. A wide double staircase passes beneath an enormous brass chandelier, welcoming people into the doctor's waiting room.

Austin also maintains a woodworking shop in the building's basement, where he practices his avocation of furniture refinishing. He reports hearing footsteps overhead while alone in the building. The first few times this occurred, he left his project and explored the upper levels for intruders, hammer in hand as protection. These sojourns revealed no one else inside the building. After the first three or four times, Austin decided to brush them aside and get on with his work.

The dental staff has dubbed this spirit "Willie." Austin, while maintaining his skepticism, explains that staff members believe Willie was a student at the school who continues to haunt the old building, as it was the one place he felt safe. What drew Austin to this conclusion he did not elaborate.

He also speaks of a young patient who claimed to see the ghost of a little girl in a pink dress sitting on the stairs beneath the brass chandelier. He pointed the girl out to his mother, who saw nothing. Suddenly, the boy pointed to another flight of stairs on the opposite end of the lobby, claiming that the girl was now sitting there, looking at him. Finally, according to the boy, the girl stood up, crossed the lobby once more and headed down the main stairs and out the front door, which he heard slam. The mother heard and saw nothing.

This could be the imaginings of a young child, perhaps trying to scare his mother into leaving before he, himself, had to brave the dentist's chair. Then again, they say children are much more open to the paranormal, not yet jaded and having learned—or been taught—to pretend it does not exist.

The Samuel Strong School has been investigated by several paranormal groups. Vicky Jellison, an investigator with Hart City Paranormal, captured electronic voice phenomena (EVPs) in various parts of the building. She was also once in possession of a photo that purportedly showed the ghost of a janitor looking out of one of the boarded-up third-story windows. She gave this photo to Dr. Austin. Unfortunately, the whereabouts of this photo are currently unknown.

Neither child spirit has been identified with any accuracy. Willie's name is the invention of the dental staff. Even the name of the janitor has been lost to time, alas.

Could Samuel Strong himself be haunting the old building? For someone who earned the privilege of having a school and a street named after him, his life has gone largely uncelebrated. There was not even an obituary in the local papers. That may be enough to make anyone restless.

13

NICE PLACE FOR A PICNIC

In October 2018, Ruthmere Museum, the 1910 mansion where I work, held a fundraising event at Grace Lawn Cemetery. After a Historic Cemetery Walk earlier in the evening, paying guests joined SPEAR in a paranormal investigation. Twenty guests took part, divided into four teams, each led by a trained investigator. Cofounder Jesse James and I were joined by my friend Marcia VanZile and her nephew Aaron VanZile as team leaders.

Prior to launching the investigation, Ruthmere went through all the appropriate channels with the City of Elkhart to get permission to be at Grace Lawn after sundown. The head of the cemetery board, Diana Strickland*, said there were no reports of paranormal activity but nonetheless gave us permission to investigate.

Situated on a bluff overlooking the Elkhart River, Grace Lawn Cemetery has quite a history. It is the final resting place of many of the city's earliest citizens and many of its most prominent. Among those buried there are Albert (1847–1924) and Elizabeth (1850–1924) Beardsley, the original owners of Ruthmere Mansion, as well as their daughter Ruth, who died in 1881 at eight months old. The Beardsleys both died in 1924, about four months apart, of natural causes, though some romantics choose to believe that Albert pined away after the love of his life passed.

Albert was the cofounder of Miles Laboratories, creators of such popular household products as Alka-Seltzer (invented by Albert's nephew Hub around 1931), One A Day Vitamins, Bactine and SOS Soap Pads. Albert's

Grace Lawn Cemetery front gates, donated by Elizabeth Beardsley in 1918.

cofounders, Dr. Franklin Miles and George E. Compton, are also buried at Grace Lawn. In 1918, Elizabeth Beardsley funded the intricate wrought-iron gates that flank the cemetery's main entrance to this day.

Grace Lawn is the oldest existing cemetery in Elkhart, established in 1855, about twenty-three years after Dr. Havilah Beardsley (1795–1856), Albert's uncle, founded the town. Havilah is buried at Grace Lawn, having been moved from the previous unnamed burial ground in 1864. John M. Rice, Eli Conley and John and Anna Evans sold land to the city, in three separate parcels, for use as a cemetery. The Evanses are buried here. Charles Beardsley surveyed the land for the cemetery, gratis. As a thank-you, the city named the new cemetery in honor of his daughter Grace Clark. Both are buried here.

As of 1999, according to city records, more than 12,600 people lie eternally at Grace Lawn, including at least one hundred Civil War soldiers. Perhaps most notable of these is the youngest enlisted Union soldier in American history, Avery Brown, who joined the Union army as a drummer at the age of eight. (Amazingly, a nine-year-old drummer, George Coleman, is buried at nearby Rice Cemetery. He was a few months older than Brown.) After being dragged home by his distraught mother, Avery reenlisted at the age of eleven, serving until the end of the war in 1865. He died of natural causes in 1929.

Located in almost the exact center of Grace Lawn is the impressive Beardsley family mausoleum, where Albert, Elizabeth and Ruth, among others, lie. This Romanesque, domed, marble structure, reminiscent of Thomas Jefferson's Monticello on a much smaller scale, is a beautiful and even pleasant place to be. The interior is colorfully lit by a large painted-glass window covered in elegant iron filigree. There are some oddities within, however. A large, irregular slab of marble, about four feet long, leans against one of the enclosed tombs, its origins unexplained. There are no missing pieces from any of the three-high banks of tombs and no visible repairs to the dome, floor or walls. Its very presence is an anomaly.

Most peculiar of all, a curious wrought-iron table and chairs stand in the center of the Beardsley mausoleum, a heavy majolica vase on top of the table. Did family members come here for Sunday picnics? It was not uncommon in the Victorian era to picnic at a cemetery—but inside the mausoleum? That seems a tad creepy. Despite these quirks, the Beardsley sepulcher is actually a peaceful little nook to spend eternity—or even just a few minutes.

While visiting the cemetery on Memorial Day 2021 with Marcia, I took some photos of the mausoleum and grounds, including those shown here. One interior shot of the mausoleum shows the window, but it also shows a couple of anomalies, one of which I can explain, one I can't. In the lower right of the picture is a diagonal row of what appear to be lights. I must emphasize that this picture was actually taken from outside, with the camera held up to the glass of the door. Therefore, I can conclude that this string of "lights" is actually the reflection of the zipper on my motorcycle jacket.

That shimmering halo around the window is an anomaly caused by light pouring in through the colored glass, creating some sort of artifact through the camera lens.

In the lower left-hand corner, however, is something a little harder to explain. There appears to be a large, oblong blob of light. This could be a fingerprint on the glass. I'm perfectly willing to accept that theory, except that I didn't see any prints.

In addition to the prestigious company presently interred at Grace Lawn, there are quite a few bodies that no longer rest here. Due to the erosive powers of the Elkhart River, much of the cemetery's western edge has been washed away over the decades, taking an unknown number of corpses with it. Certainly being swept away by a river might be cause for eternal unrest.

Beardsley mausoleum, interior, showing unexplained light anomaly in lower-left corner.

Efforts have been made to shore up the cliff, but who knows how long before another crop goes drifting on their way to Lake Michigan?

With so many prominent people buried here, you would think *someone* might linger. But that begs the question, "Why would they?" If ghosts are supposed to haunt places that were significant during their lifetimes—a house, a business, the place they died—why would they choose to linger in a cemetery, which likely played little or no role in their lives until *after* they died? Your guess is as good as mine. It may explain why Diana Strickland said she knew of no activity. Nevertheless, SPEAR opted to give it a try—for charity, of course.

It was a cool, crisp October night, ideal conditions for an outdoor investigation. The ground was dry, the sky was cloudless and the partial moon provided enough light to enhance the interior of the cemetery, where no electric lampposts stood. A light breeze wasn't even strong enough to lift fallen autumn leaves off the ground.

We broke up into four teams, each taking a variety of equipment. For two hours, we made our way counterclockwise around the cemetery, each group keeping well apart to avoid audio contamination. After some time, I was starting to think Diana was right. My team got no results: no readings on our EMF (electromagnetic field) detectors and no photos of anything other than trees and tombstones.

At one point, I did spot an odd streak of light moving across the path about twenty feet away. I tracked it with my eyes for about fifteen feet before it disappeared, too quickly for me to alert anyone. No one else on my team saw it. Aaron's team was about eighty feet ahead; Marcia's and Jesse's teams were on the other side of the cemetery grounds. What that light might have been I cannot say. Logic dictates that I put it down to the reflection of someone's flashlight on a row of tombstones. But whose? No one in my group was aiming a light in that direction. And why didn't it blink in and out, as it would if it really was reflecting off a series of unattached surfaces? No idea.

Battery drain, the sudden loss of power from batteries, is a frequent occurrence during a paranormal investigation and may be something we experienced that night. Some believe spirits can draw energy from batteries and other sources of energy, natural or artificial, to help them manifest. An EMF detector can allegedly reveal the presence of a ghost.

I radioed Aaron at one point but got no response. It was only when we were packing up to leave that he said he heard nothing. All the equipment had fresh batteries at the start of the investigation—standard procedure— so there is no logical explanation as to why his, and only his, walkie-talkie should go dead. There might easily be a mechanical fault in play, but then again, there might not.

About thirty minutes before we were to wrap up, however, Marcia radioed that her team was getting some results with their EMF detector and the spirit box. We converged on the northeast quadrant of the cemetery, where one of Marcia's team, Natalie Imrie*, was conducting an EVP session with her aunt, Mary Boarder*, who lay in rest at Grace Lawn. The EMF detector rested firmly on top of Mary's gravestone, while Natalie, Marcia, and everyone else stood back several feet. They had a video camera aimed directly at the stone and the EMF.

Sure enough, as Natalie asked questions, the colored lights on the detector lit up, seemingly in response to the yes-or-no questions being posed. Following established protocol, positive answers yielded lights, negative answers did not. As we watched, we grew increasingly excited at the apparent interaction taking place between Natalie and her aunt.

Natalie's questions were fairly straightforward. "Are you Mary Boarder?" "Do you know who I am?" "Are you happy?" Certainly nothing misleading or confusing.

I made certain to examine the vicinity for power lines. A previous event with T~NIPS at a cemetery in Constantine, Michigan, yielded some embarrassed laughs when one team discovered they were standing under high-tension lines while seemingly getting remarkable responses to their questions. Only when they looked up did they realize exactly why they seemed to have such a chatty spirit in their midst. Needless to say, we had to toss that incident aside. I wanted to be sure no such circumstances applied to Natalie's success. While there were telephone wires running along the edge of the cemetery, they were at least thirty feet away and unlikely to cause any interference with the EMF detector.

After about fifteen minutes, we decided to call it an evening. We were supposed to be in the cemetery only until midnight, and we still had to pack away all the equipment and award our guests their "certificates of bravery" for surviving a night among the ghosts of Grace Lawn Cemetery, or for being a good sport while they felt foolish standing in the dark on a chilly Saturday night talking to air, whichever the case may be. Everyone seemed to have a good time, though.

The next step was evidence analysis. As had always been the case with SPEAR, I took the digital recorders home with me, and Jesse took the DVR system. I've never trusted my eyesight enough to stare at a TV screen, unblinking, for hours on end without missing something. My hearing, however, is very acute from years of analyzing and dissecting music. Jesse and I would spend a couple of weeks going over our evidence—we both worked full-time jobs and lived in different states, so analysis would take a while—and then compare notes once we were done. It is Jesse's results more than anything that make me question whether or not Diana Strickland is right about there being no activity at Grace Lawn.

Nothing of interest came from any of the digital recorders. Not a single audible response. From Marcia's recorder, we heard Natalie asking questions of her aunt Mary, of course. There were no audible responses there either, sadly, except the chatter from the spirit box, a device that scans radio frequencies at high speed and broadcasts whatever it picks up. With the large number of radio stations in the Elkhart / South Bend area, however, it was bound to pick up countless signals, even if only for a split second each.[*] That meant we would have to rely on the video evidence. Remember, the DVR camera was aimed directly at Mary Boarder's tombstone with the EMF detector resting on top. We had all seen the lights flashing on the little black device as Natalie spoke to her aunt.

Imagine our surprise when the DVR camera showed nothing from the EMF detector! The tombstone was clearly visible, as was the detector itself, but not a single flash of light emanated from the device. The camera's microphone recorded Natalie's questions and the comments of the other team members as the EMF "spoke" on Mary's behalf. But not a blip or a wink to be seen. How to explain that? Twenty-odd people watched the EMF detector flashing in perfect timing to the questions, but the camera showed zilch.

_____

[*] The theory behind the spirit box is that ghosts can use radio frequencies to communicate. But how do you differentiate between the stray words of disc jockeys the spirit box emits and a voice from the Other Side? Besides, the white noise generated by nonbroadcasting frequencies is loud enough to drown out all but the strongest signals.

Is it possible the camera malfunctioned in some way? If so, why did it show such clear images of everything else? It could be that the lights on the EMF were not bright enough for the night-vision camera to pick up, but that seems unlikely given that the lights would have been brighter than their surroundings, including the black plastic case of the detector itself. What else could have caused this oddity? Without any audio responses from Aunt Mary or other entities that may have been present, no one can say that Natalie Imrie truly made contact with anyone from Beyond. I'd like to think she did, but wishing does not make it so.

Does this mean Grace Lawn Cemetery is haunted? Based on our experience, I do not have enough evidence to say yes. All I know is that we experienced something inexplicable that October night in 2018. Future investigations might reveal more compelling evidence. The skeptic in me says it is not haunted. But what about those blinking lights? Can twenty-plus people, tightly grouped together and looking in the same direction, all be mistaken about the same thing?

14

ALL GOOD THINGS MUST COME TO AN END...EVEN ROBBIE

L ike most cities in America, if not around the world, Elkhart has lost many of its beautiful, historic buildings. The Century Club on Main Street is no exception. Indeed, all that remains of this Romanesque structure are a handful of postcards for sale online. Built in 1898 by Herbert E. Bucklen, the Century Club was a traditional "gentlemen's club," where the wealthy barons of business could mingle, exchange ideas and boast of their lucre.

Herbert Bucklen was born in Herkimer County, New York, on July 19, 1848. A medical doctor by training, he relocated to Elkhart, Indiana, in the early 1870s and began amassing his fortune through the invention and sale of a patent medicine he called Arnica Salve. Arnica was an instant sensation, paving the way for many imitations over the years.

On August 16, 1877, Bucklen wed Bertha Electa Redfield of Cass County, Michigan. The couple settled in Elkhart and raised three children, Harley, Charlotte and Herbert Jr.

Bucklen's success in the pharmaceutical game allowed him to speculate on other investments, most notably railroads. In 1894, he began construction on the Elkhart & Western Railroad Company, connecting his new hometown with Mishawaka in neighboring St. Joseph County. Because of his success with Arnica, the railroad gained the nickname the "Arnica Salve Line." The E&W was bought by the Lake Shore & Michigan Southern in 1898, giving Bucklen's fortune another considerable boost.

Century Club, from a 1905 postcard.

Real estate also beckoned. Bucklen purchased the 1863 Clifton House Hotel and began extensive restorations. In addition, he owned a number of properties in Chicago, where he also had a residence. In 1889, the Clifton House was renamed the Hotel Bucklen, garnering a place in Elkhart history. He also constructed the Bucklen Opera House. (Both buildings were said to be haunted.) Sadly, both the hotel and the opera house, like the Century Club, have disappeared from the landscape.

Bucklen departed this world on January 10, 1917, passing away at his Chicago residence. Bertha died on November 16, 1929, in Ontwa, Michigan, not far from where she was born. Both are buried in God's Half Acre Cemetery in Edwardsburg, Michigan, just over the state line from Elkhart.

Among the employees at the Century Club was, allegedly, a caretaker named Robbie. No last name has come down for this man, who was said to be mildly mentally challenged. The existence of Robbie, therefore, remains unconfirmed.

Exactly when Robbie died is unrecorded, but he made a lasting home for himself on the third floor of the club. His ghost was reported to dance around the top-floor ballroom, where footsteps and other noises were frequently heard. Lights turned on by themselves on many occasions when no one was in the building. Doors opened and closed of their own volition. Some club members even claimed to feel Robbie's breath on them, an unnerving sensation, to be sure.

Over the years, the Century Club changed names, owners and purposes. The original club gave way to the Atherton Club, and, in succession, the Moose Lodge, the electronics division of band-instrument manufacturer C.G. Conn and several more.

Eventually, the building's usefulness ran its course. It was razed in 1986 to make way for the Valley American Bank parking lot. The site is still occupied by a lot today, but it seems as though Robbie, deprived of his eternal home, has moved on.

15

TO THE MANOR BORN

S usan South lives in her childhood home on St. Joseph Manor in Elkhart. Her parents, Dale and Mary, bought the white-sided Colonial Revival home in 1969 and lived there until about 1980, when Susan was twenty-four. Susan bought it back in 1990 and has lived there ever since. But she is not alone.

"I have no idea how many spirits are in the house. I've had encounters throughout the years," Susan says. "I just know they're there."

The beautiful house, located in one of Elkhart's most affluent neighborhoods, was built in 1929, according to city directories, but multiple real estate websites date it to 1922. One of the more prolific stories about the house is that the original owner, Van Kipka (1890–1931), after losing all his money (perhaps in the stock market crash of 1929), became despondent over not being able to complete his dream house and hanged himself inside. According to Susan, this is nonsense, nothing more than a folktale. Interestingly, Van and his wife, Gertrude, shared a birthday, both born on St. Patrick's Day, March 17, in 1890 and 1893, respectively. It would seem the luck of the Irish was not with him, though. Van died at the age of forty-three. Gertrude sold the house in 1934. She continued living in Elkhart, finally passing away in 1981, almost fifty years after her husband. Both are buried in Rice Cemetery, Elkhart.

Gertrude Kipka sold the property to a couple from Minnesota, Henry Benjamin "Ben" Williams and his wife, Besse Mott Williams. Ben, like Van

Susan South's house, where a fastidious ghost makes her annoyance clearly known.

Kipka, was born in 1890; Besse in 1891. They lived in the house on St. Joseph Manor for more than twenty-five years. Ben died in 1960, followed by Besse in 1962. They, too, are buried at Rice Cemetery.

Charlie and Renata O'Donnell* purchased the home about a year after Besse's passing but stayed for only four years, leaving the house in 1967. After sitting vacant for a year, the house was purchased by Susan's parents, Dale and Mary South.

According to Susan, Renata O'Donnell saw the ghost of the original builder, Van Kipka, descending the stairs and going out the front door. How she identified him is unknown. One night, she claimed to hear noises downstairs while she was in bed. The next morning, all the kitchen cabinets were empty and their contents had been stacked neatly on the counters. Perhaps the kitchen was not arranged to Gertrude Kipka's standards!

After living elsewhere for a decade, Susan managed to purchase the house and continues living there today. Over the last three decades, she has had multiple experiences. "A couple of times I saw shadows in my bedroom. Not dark, black ones, just gray."

"I've heard conversations," she adds, "and the television wasn't on. And I listen and just go back to what I was doing. It's usually about the time I'm relaxing and getting ready to go to sleep, you know, and I'll hear conversations downstairs." She has not been able to make out what is being said, or whether the voices are male or female. But, as long as they don't try to engage her in the dialogue, she is content to let them chat.

A level-headed woman, Susan does not let mere noises upset her. "You've got to differentiate between the sounds of an old house, and I'm pretty good about that."

She says she felt a presence blow into her ear one night while she was lying in bed. She has also seen "little cloudy things" that her cat Sadie would chase.

"The most frequent thing that happens is I feel them following me upstairs. And I know it's not just….Unless you've felt that feeling, you don't understand it. And I run upstairs and I say, 'Back off!'"

Susan claims not to fear the entities in the house, saying they never felt malevolent. Mischievous, perhaps, but not evil. Until one night in 2021, that is, when she found her other cat, Luna, at the bottom of the basement stairs, cowering in terror. Several attempts to summon the cat failed, and Susan was finally able to understand what was frightening her. In as commanding a voice as she could, she demanded the entities leave her Luna alone. Since then, she says with confidence that whatever was there has now gone, or at least has continued to lay low after the scolding.

Susan South has no immediate plans to sell the house she now shares with other family members. After so many years of living in relative harmony with her unseen housemates, it would be a shame for them to drive her away now, especially if they took her chastising to heart.

16

A NURSE'S DUTY NEVER ENDS

M any hospitals around the world can claim paranormal activity. This is not at all surprising given the amount of trauma that occurs within. People die in hospitals every day. How many of them stick around afterward? Not just patients, but doctors and nurses may linger, perhaps out of a sense of duty. Or maybe out of a sense of guilt. The Western Infirmary in Glasgow, Scotland, is allegedly haunted by the ghost of a brain surgeon who refused to operate on a poor artist. Shortly after, the artist fell to his death down a flight of stairs at the hospital. The surgeon, out of remorse, haunts the infirmary to this day.

The now-disappeared Clark Street Hospital in Elkhart has an interesting history, one that does not lend itself readily to ghost stories. But stories there are, nonetheless.

Hannah Whiting was born in New Boston, New Hampshire, on December 31, 1817. She married James E. Clark in 1839 in Johnson, Vermont. The couple relocated to Elkhart, Indiana, in 1845. James set up in business as a harness dealer, eventually amassing a fortune of some $30,000 by the time of his death in 1863. The couple had two children, both of whom died young, leaving Hannah to inherit her husband's fortune.

Mr. and Mrs. Clark, longtime friends of the Kellogg brothers of breakfast cereal fame, lived in a wood-frame house at 111 North Clark Street. Records do not show if the street was named after the wealthy couple or if it already bore that happy name. Either way, in 1899, Hannah Clark bequeathed a large section of her property to the City of Elkhart with the stipulation that the land be used for the construction of a new hospital. A further condition was that Hannah be allowed to live in her home until her death.

A two-story Queen Anne Gothic structure in red brick was built adjacent to the frame house, the two joined into a single structure. Hannah did, indeed, live in the original home until her death on December 11, 1900. At some point in Elkhart history the buildings along Clark Street were renumbered, the hospital designated as 126 North Clark Street.

The Homeopathic Hospital, as it was originally called, officially opened on July 1, 1899. The original board of directors consisted of Drs. Albert Fisher, W.H. Thomas, Porter Turner, Andrew Mumaw and C.D. Goodrich. Turner was a former mayor of Elkhart. He and his wife eventually moved into the original frame house, where Mrs. Turner cooked for the patients. The first matron, in charge of the nurses, was a Mrs. Nichols, a graduate of the Hahneman Hospital School of Nursing in Chicago. Miss N.G. Collins, a Johns Hopkins–trained nurse, taught three student nurses in the first year: Maude Kellington, Evelyn Skinner and Dora Bechtel.

Clark Street Hospital, now gone, from an antique postcard. *Courtesy of RoseMary McDaniel.*

Facilities were always limited, with many patients being sent home immediately after surgery. At its peak, the Homeopathic Hospital could not accommodate more than seventeen patients at a time.

In 1904, the facility was renamed the Clark Hospital in memory of Hannah Clark, and the board of directors was revamped. Dr. Turner was named vice-president and manager, and Thomas was named president. Fisher remained and was joined by A.P. Kent and attorney J.M. Van Fleet. Bertha Seibert, a graduate of the Illinois Training School for Nurses, was named superintendent of nurses. Porter Turner eventually started his own hospital on Second Street. In time, Maude Kellington joined the nursing staff there.

Also in 1904, Clark Hospital began its own nursing school, graduating two students in 1905: Mary I. Whiteman and Isabel Russ Hall.

Seibert left the hospital in 1909 and was replaced by Agnes Leiber. She served as superintendent of nurses for only a few months before being dismissed for failing to maintain standards among the nursing students. She was replaced on July 31, 1909, by Agnes Maloney. At that time, the hospital boasted fourteen beds, five student nurses and a "trained" nurse in charge, presumably Maloney.

In the early years, nurses lived at home and were called in to work as needed. For a few years, they were housed in the hospital itself until the nearby Nurses' Home was constructed in 1913. At that time, the nursing school was transferred to Elkhart General Hospital, as were all the patients. Clark Street Hospital closed its doors on July 31, 1913. The nursing school continued on at Elkhart General until 1932.

With the departure of the hospital staff, the building at 126 North Clark Street sat empty for three years. It was finally sold in 1916 for $3,115 and was converted into apartments, a purpose it served for the next one hundred years or so.

Over the decades, residents in the apartment building claimed to hear agonized screams and other chilling sounds. Many reports of a stern-faced woman in a white nurse's uniform were told and retold. Who this dutiful nurse may be is anyone's guess. Could she be Bertha Seibert, still tending to long-departed patients only she can see? Perhaps it's the angry specter of Agnes Leiber, fired for dereliction of duty. Could it be Hannah Clark herself? Or perhaps it is Mrs. Turner, the kindly woman who cooked for the ailing patients.

Stories are all that remain of the Clark Street Hospital and its ghostly residents. The building was razed in 2019 to make way for Elkhart Health

& Aquatics. Indeed, Clark Street itself barely still exists. The new aquatic center and its extensive grounds occupy most of the site that was once a residential backstreet in turn-of-the-century Elkhart, and the street is now little more than the entrance to the parking lot. It appears the ghosts have disappeared along with the historic hospital.

17

THE HOUSE THAT NELLIE BUILT... AND NEVER LEFT

WINCHESTER MANSION, ELKHART

Virtually every town in America, if not the world, has one house—*that* house—the locals point to with awe and caution. "Yeah, *that's* the house I was telling you about." It's the staple of many a scary movie. Such houses are usually old, ornate, dilapidated and undeniably spooky. It's almost passé.

Elkhart certainly has its share, regrettably, of old, abandoned houses. But the house everyone talks about around here—*that* house—is far from forlorn. The Winchester Mansion at 529 South Second Street is beautiful, well preserved, remarkably unaltered by time and notoriously haunted. Built in 1905 for local banker William Herrick Knickerbocker and his wife, Nellie Winchester, this brooding structure in dark brown brick and white trim looms over downtown Elkhart, one of the few mansions south of the St. Joseph River still standing, virtually unaltered.

"I love that the integrity of the property remains," says new owner Chris Baiker. "Every time we come across something that hasn't changed, we go, 'Oooh!' All said, especially given the fact that a lot of people in downtown Elkhart just didn't appreciate these homes, and they tore 'em down or gutted them or whatever, this somehow survived. And that amazes me."

It's obvious that this house has been loved for its entire life. It stands as a monument to the gilded age of Elkhart, much like Ruthmere. Interestingly,

Winchester Mansion from across Second Street. Note the light in the center dormer window.

the two houses share a sisterhood of sorts. It is well documented that Nellie Knickerbocker and Elizabeth Beardsley were close friends, cohorts. Both women were active in the women's suffrage movement of the early twentieth century. Both were active in local education services, having worked jointly to bring the first bookmobile to Elkhart in the 1910s. Most notably, both women suffered a tragic loss in their younger years.

Born in 1863 in Allen, Michigan (the precise date is not known), Nellie Winchester seemed destined to marry into money. Although not connected to the Winchesters of rifle fame—and thus no connection to the famous Winchester Mystery House in San Jose, California, also notoriously haunted—Nellie came from a wealthy family. As is often the case, money marries money and begets…more money. Nellie married William Herrick Knickerbocker on November 29, 1883, in Elkhart.

William's mother, Eliza Herrick, was originally from Elkhart and, as a young girl, moved with her mother to Putnam County, New York. Eliza married Jacob Knickerbocker (born March 17, 1853, in Rhineland, New

York) and proceeded to raise three sons and a daughter: William, Calvin, Gene and Carrie. Jacob Knickerbocker passed away in 1867. Following his death, Eliza relocated her brood to Elkhart to be with family.

After only a few years in Indiana, however, Eliza moved to California, taking her three youngest children with her. William, the oldest, was left in the care of Eliza's sister Euphemia Stephens. In 1872, at the age of nineteen, William went to work for the St. Joseph Valley Bank, eventually working his way up to cashier. He left that job to work as cashier at First National Bank in 1886. As it happens, Nellie's father, Charles Winchester, was president of First National, so we can imply a certain amount of nepotism in William's rise to the top. He was elected town clerk in 1873 and also served as the Dean of Indiana Bankers. He succeeded as president of First National at Charles's death in 1917, remaining in that lofty post until retiring in 1931.

In 1905, having amassed quite a fortune, William and Nellie built the sprawling house at the corner of Second and Harrison Streets, only two blocks north of the Elkhart Railroad Depot. William had a vested interest in the railroad industry in town and liked to be close to his assets.

At some point, around 1890—though the dates are far from certain—Nellie apparently gave birth to a son, Howard, at least according to a 1900 *Elkhart Truth* article about the couple. Nellie was very guarded about her personal life, so much of her story remains speculation. Her own obituary, as well as William's, makes no mention of a child having been born, much less dying in infancy. This, however, might explain why Nellie and Elizabeth Beardsley were so close. Elizabeth lost her only child, Ruth, at eight months in 1881.

Indeed, the two women's lives share a remarkable number of parallels. Both came from affluent Elkhart families. Both married wealthy business tycoons from out of state. Both were petite, standing only about five feet tall. Both lived in grand mansions known for lavish parties. Both fought for thc votc for women. Both lived with their husbands, more or less alone, in their lush homes. Both drove Milburn electric cars (Nellie's is now in the Ruthmere Museum collection). Both lost their only child in infancy.

Nellie found herself even more alone when her husband passed away on December 3, 1937. Like Albert Beardsley of Ruthmere, William died at home. Like Elizabeth Beardsley, Nellie was also fated to die at home, joining her husband on March 3, 1947. After a lingering heart illness, she was found sitting in her favorite chair by a servant when he reported to work that morning.

More than the extravagant entertaining or the beautiful house she created, Nellie Winchester Knickerbocker was known for her eccentricities. She was infamous for her driving habits. Stories tell of her Milburn stopped in the middle of Main Street while Nellie inspected, up close, items in store windows. The good folks of Elkhart knew of this peculiarity and that it would serve them naught to honk or protest. The general response was simply to drive around her car and get on with living.

Like Elizabeth, Nellie was known as a "character," a feisty old woman who lived life by her own rules and damn the rest! One of the more persistent rumors about her, as outlined in the same 1900 article from the *Truth*, is that Nellie slept in a coffin every night. However, the article clarifies this folktale by emphasizing that while Nellie did indeed keep a coffin in the room now known as the Peacock Room, she did not repose in it. She kept it tucked behind an Oriental screen, out of sight. She purchased the elegant coffin out of fear. Nellie was not liked by her husband's family, and she lived her later years in the firm belief that at her death, they would undoubtedly choose to bury her in something shoddy and cheap. So she chose to head them off by purchasing her own eternal furniture. She is now entombed in her elegant casket beside William in Grace Lawn Cemetery. There is no record of where her son, Howard, is buried.

In 1944, three years before her death, Nellie sold the house to Ernest C. Cripe of Goshen, Indiana, though she continued to live there until her death. Cripe owned the house until 1953, when he sold it to the Juhl Advertising Company. Juhl remained in the house for twenty-five years, vacating it in 1978.

The mansion stood empty for a full decade before being converted into banqueting rooms in 1988. At this time, necessary repairs were carried out, but, as Chris Baiker points out, the integrity of the home remained remarkably intact.

In 2004, the Winchester Mansion became devoted to helping children. The upstairs was divided into office space—again without altering the structure, aside from an unsightly column built in what Chris and his wife, Phalene Leichtman, call the Blue Room. The column, which serves no structural purpose, houses a bevy of electrical outlets. Chris and Phalene intend to remove this column in the fullness of time. The southern half of the house served as a therapist's clinic for children, while the northern half was devoted to child-support collection services. Chris and Phalene bought the house in the early fall of 2021. As of this writing, they have lived in the house for just a few months, having spent the previous three months cleaning and getting the house ready to serve as their home. They also intend to use the sprawling house as an event center for weddings and the like, as well as a bed-and-breakfast. With a combined twenty years and more in the restaurant and catering trade, Phalene and Chris seem well suited to the task ahead.

Of the Blue Room,* Chris says, "We established the room that is rumored to be one of the most active in terms of the paranormal activity as the first guest room we've been able to get up and running." Since he and Phalene took ownership of the mansion, several people have stayed in the Blue Room, including Chris's children from his first marriage. "So that room has been thoroughly gone through. And out of the blue the other night, I discover a blue marble on the floor just outside the closet door where we would walk all the time. I have to approach it skeptically, right? So I immediately reached out to the kids. They're teenagers, they don't have marbles. It's in the kitchen now. I didn't want to dispose of it. That was…kind of a creepy thing."

Apports—objects that appear in a location with no obvious explanation—are not uncommon in the annals of paranormal literature. Such things are often accompanied by other prankish behavior. As mentioned before, Nellie Knickerbocker was known as a prankster, so it is easy to imagine her depositing that marble as a subtle sign to let people know she is still around.

"Nellie is definitely very playful," Chris continues. "I've had things misplaced that were distinctly placed. I'll sweep up, set the dustpan down and then go do something, come back, and the dustpan's not where I left it."

Phalene, an Elkhart native in her own right, adds: "I typically use what was the master bathroom. There's just like a stand-still toilet roll dispenser. I like [the paper] to go over the top, and every day I go to the bathroom and it's *under*. And I'm like, 'What the hell?' So I asked him the other day, 'Chris, do you keep flipping the toilet paper over?' And he said, 'No, I don't even use that bathroom.'"

Phalene also relates the story of a previous owner who complained of newspapers and magazines disappearing from one of the upstairs offices and ending up down the laundry chute! Again, they lay the blame bemusedly at Nellie's feet.

---

* Why is it that Blue Rooms always seem to be the most haunted? Inveraray Castle in Scotland has a haunted Blue Room, as does the White House in Washington, D.C. England's legendary Borley Rectory, subject of extensive paranormal investigation by Harry Price in the first half of the twentieth century, also had a Blue Room, which was the focus of its ghostly history. Indeed, three rectors, including father and son Henry and Harry Bull, died in the Blue Room at Borley.

Or perhaps not so bemusedly. According to multiple sources, both oral and written, the previous owner sold the mansion because he grew tired of coming to work every morning and finding his office (the Blue Room again) tossed about as if a cyclone had hit. During the closing ceremony at the realtor's office—and this story has been confirmed by the realtor herself—the previous owner offered to help Chris and Phalene acclimate to their new home by taking care of some minor projects, showing them how alarms and other devices worked and the like. However, according to Phalene and the realtor, the minute the paperwork was signed and the transfer was complete, the seller severed all ties with the Winchester Mansion, the realtor and the home's new owners. "He ghosted *us!*" Chris says with a chuckle.

Chris and Phalene laugh joyfully about the goings-on in their new old home, a sign that they do not see any threats in the house. Phalene says: "The back entryway, where you came in"—which I had told her felt active to me—"that light is on a switch, but it's on a motion sensor. And so at night, we let the dogs out, and we have to turn it on and turn it back off. So the light will go on before we go out, just to make sure, you know, the coast is clear. And, at night, every time before we go to bed, we set the alarm, lock that gate up, and the light stays on. It's very weird….And it will stay on for, like, a half hour. Normally it shuts off in, like, a minute or whatever….I feel like it's almost like someone watching over us."

The comfortable feeling, however, is not necessarily mutual. There have been several reports over the years of Christmas trees moving and even falling over during office holiday parties when no one was near them.

Chris's children came to visit the house shortly after he and Phalene took possession. "I would say there's a lot of energy in the basement," Chris explains. "That's probably where I feel it the most. Our son, who's fifteen, says to me, 'You know, this house feels pretty good, but that door, that's not good.'" Chris points to a large metal door leading into the main basement chamber. "I feel it," he continues. "It's a palpable energy when you go into that cellar, and it's not just because it's a cellar."

Much of the recent activity centers on the kids' visit. Chris continues: "The other night, after hearing a very loud noise in our bedroom that woke me, startled me…I heard footsteps running down the hallway, down the stairs. I thought it was one of the kids. I pop up and there was nobody there."

"One of the things that happened to us that stands out the most," he goes on, "is we had Phalene's nephew over, who's seven. This was before

Above: Main stairs, Winchester Mansion, where Chris Baiker has heard footsteps descending at night.

Opposite: Back stairs, Winchester Mansion, where a ghostly man in work clothes lingers.

we moved in and we were just here, doing something. And he's kind of wandering around the house. Then, when we left, as we got into the car, I looked up and saw the attic light was on. It hadn't been on when we pulled in, and so now it was on."

"We didn't want to say anything," Phalene inserts, "because we didn't want to freak him out."

Chris continues: "Yeah, so we just looked at each other with that—'the light's on.' Adam*, unsolicited, said something to the effect of, 'Are spirits real?' All my hair stood up at that point!"

Indeed, the attic lights come on by themselves practically every day. Chris admits he has not had an electrician out to inspect them, so this may yet be disproved.

Nellie is not the only apparition seen in the Winchester Mansion. Phalene explains that a former therapist who worked in the building saw the figure of a man. "She was leaving the house one night. She was in the kitchen, grabbing her bag and stuff. She walked around the corner to walk down

the [servants'] stairs to leave, and there was a man standing there in, like, a work uniform. So it wasn't Nellie, it was definitely a man. She said she kind of blinked and took a step back around the corner, then went back and he wasn't there."

There have also been reports of a child seen standing in one of the upstairs windows. Chris even had a conversation with a local police officer about this. Could this be one of the therapy patients who spent some time in the Blue Room?

"Previous to us owning this place," Phalene says, "the people that owned it ran a child-psychiatry / therapist's office out of it. It was also used as a child-support office. There's definitely heavier energy because of what the building has been used for."

Chris and Phalene have yet to see anything too shocking. "It was a little disappointing—I know it sounds crazy—that we haven't seen more apparitions in the house," Chris proclaims with a little laugh. "I've seen two outside. One was this woman figure out here." He gestures to the dining room window overlooking Harrison Street. "And then I saw her through *this* window [overlooking Second Street]. It struck me as odd because she was dressed all in black with a hood up. As she passed by that window, I went to the other and she was *gone!* And you have to either cross the street here or walk in front of the house. So there's nowhere to go.

"Then I saw a gentleman pass between the houses late at night. Again, just sort of…gone. Not before my eyes. It went out of sight from one window and then never reappeared. I guess it could've been a person, but I don't know where they could've went or how quickly they could've got away."

Could William and Nellie both haunt the Winchester Mansion? While most of the experiences have been light, even friendly, some incidents have not been so comforting. As Phalene was getting into bed one night, "I felt like someone sat on the bed. So I, like, scooted my foot over to Chris's foot in case he was moving. He wasn't, and I just thought, 'Not tonight. I'm too tired.'"

They jointly tell of an experience they shared just before my visit. Chris heard a loud crash downstairs. Phalene was upstairs and heard nothing. Chris's subsequent investigation turned up nothing amiss. About fifteen minutes later, Phalene heard an equally loud crash while standing in the kitchen. Again, immediate investigation revealed no disturbance.

"I came out, and the cat, Winnie, heard it too and she was looking at me like, 'What did you do?!'"

Winnie—short for Winchester but adamantly called Winnie—has a fascination with the attic. One incident freaked out Phalene in particular. Winnie disappeared. Phalene, fearing she had escaped outside, set about searching the house from bottom to top. Finally, Chris found Winnie in the attic, sitting right on the step, "totally chilled." Phalene insists, "That door was *closed!*"

Chris was decidedly unnerved by an incident that occurred a few weeks before they officially began residing in the mansion. "Before we moved in

Closet door that opened spontaneously. Several possible orbs are visible.

here, we were staying with Phalene's parents and I had to come over here one night by myself to pick up golf clubs, of all things. It was the first time either of us had been in the house alone, at night in particular. So I came in and turned the alarm off. It was, you know, pretty quiet in here. I walked into this entryway and I stood there for a moment. And I heard whispers"—he imitates a low murmur—"and I went, 'Oh, jeez! Oh, my god, don't do this to me, no, no, no. So I went upstairs, I got my golf bag, I came back down…and I heard low murmuring whispers. And I looked out and said somebody's got to be on the corner, talking. It was distinctly a woman. Nothing. And so I laughed and I texted Phalene and said, 'Well, I hate to tell you this.…'"

The fact that Chris laughs at that incident suggests he is comfortable with whatever resides in the house with him and Phalene. Both smile good-naturedly, in retrospect at least, as they recount their adventures.

Shortly after purchasing the home, they found the Winchester / Knickerbocker family plot in Grace Lawn Cemetery. "We sat there for a few and I tried to have a conversation with Nellie," Chris says. "I assured her she was welcome here as long as it stayed playful."

It seems as though Nellie is keeping her end of the bargain, at least with Phalene and Chris. All evidence points to her being displeased with businesses setting up shop in her home. If Nellie was anything like Elizabeth Beardsley, the Winchester Mansion was just that, a *home*. And even though the new owners intend to use the house as a business location, they also intend to live there full-time.

"We're the first people to live here in seventy years," Phalene points out.

Phalene Leichtman and Chris Baiker understand this house. As Chris says, "Preserving the house, caring for the house, right? I think that that goes a long way, that energy. We love this space. I think that would speak to the spirit here. We're stewards of the house."

After the interview, Chris and Phalene took me on a tour of the house for photos. A closet door, previously closed, now stood wide open. My photo picked up three distinct balls of light. Were they orbs or dust? In the attic, he pointed out the lights that go on repeatedly by themselves. As we headed back downstairs, he turned off all the lights. Then, after a few more interior shots, we headed outside. The last photo was of the front of the house from across Second Street. There, plain as day, was the attic light shining through the middle dormer window, almost as if on schedule. Skepticism aside, it does give one pause for thought.

At a Ruthmere cocktail party at the Winchester Mansion a few months later, Chris and Phalene regaled the crowd with updates on their experiences. Chris spoke of hearing doors slamming, while Phalene told how a bottle of olive oil went sailing to its doom across the kitchen. Still undaunted, since they knew of the house's reputation before signing the purchase agreement, they remain jovial about the subject. Indeed, they are counting on Winchester's reputation to draw curious guests to their bed-and-breakfast and event facility. While they make no promises that you'll experience anything other than their charming hospitality, that alone is a guarantee of a good visit.

18

WHERE DREAMS COME TRUE...
MAYBE

Hamlet saw ghosts. Ebenezer Scrooge saw ghosts. Many a ghost has materialized onstage during a performance. But hundreds of theaters worldwide claim spirits within their walls that don't show themselves only during a performance. Indeed, some thespians think it is bad luck to perform in a theater that *doesn't* claim a ghostie or two.

Elkhart's Lerner Theater is no exception, although management and staff are reticent to discuss the subject. Understandably, they want their theater to be known for its live entertainment, not for its…you get the point.

Built in 1923, the Lerner is one of the grande dames of American theater. Constructed in the Beaux-Arts style at the corner of Main and Franklin Streets in the heart of downtown, it has played host to many a famed performer over the last ten decades and counting.

Harry Edward Lerner was born on December 20, 1884, in Granger, Indiana, the son of Christopher and Magdalena Arnold Lerner. A large brood, though perhaps not by the standards of the day, the Lerner offspring consisted of five boys and two girls, Harry being the oldest. A 1910 census record lists Christopher and Lena, as his mother was known, as farmers. Harry's own marriage license application, dated November 11, 1907, bears this out. On that date, Harry married Olive Mabel Borough (1886–1970) of Portage Township, Indiana. They were blessed with two children, Jean and Harry Jr.

Lerner Theater, allegedly haunted by a former technician who died at his post of a heart attack.

Lerner began building his namesake theater at 410 South Main Street in 1923. The theater officially opened to the public on November 24, 1924, offering a mix of programs, including music, vaudeville, film and an in-house orchestra. Business took off immediately, and Lerner's fortune grew steadily.

Warner Bros. took over the Lerner in 1931, renaming it after themselves. They added an enormous, glittering marquee to the front of the building that could be seen up and down Main Street. Three years later, in 1934, the Illinois-Indiana Theater Company leased the building. A countywide competition to select a new name resulted in the building being rechristened the Elco Theatre.

The Elco was purchased in 1940 by Manta & Rose Theatres, which would own and operate it for the next twenty years. It replaced the towering marquee with a more streamlined one bearing the Elco moniker. Manta & Rose also renovated the interior of the structure, modernizing it, complete with concession stands.

In 1961, the Elco was operated by the William Miller family, which kept it running until its complete closure in 1987. The building sat empty for three years before Premier Arts, a nonprofit organization, purchased it in 1990. Along with efforts from an enthusiastic Elkhart and the National Endowment for the Arts, restoration commenced once again in 1996, returning the now-legendary old theater to its original 1923 splendor. The name Lerner Theater was reapplied, and thus it remains.

Restoration continues at the Lerner, and once again the theater hosts live entertainment, from music and standup comics to Shakespeare and beyond, perhaps even *Hamlet* with its many ghosts.

Harry Edward Lerner passed away on April 13, 1971, at the age of eighty-six, and is buried in Rice Cemetery in Elkhart. Apparently at peace, he is not the ghost supposedly seen in the theater by actors and tech crew. The ghost of the Lerner is believed to be a technician who died of a heart attack while on duty. Unfortunately, no one can put a name to the alleged man, severely undercutting the validity of the claims. The classic symptoms of eerie noises and flickering lights are reported on occasion, and a ghostly form, unidentified and unrecognizable, was once spotted in the balcony by tech crew during preparations for a performance. Past reports claim that this figure was only caught on a security camera and that staff were able to identify it as a plastic sheet draped over a tall chair.

If the stories about the Lerner are not true, why would anyone go to the trouble of making them up? Several reasons suggest themselves. No one can doubt the allure of publicity, unless you have something genuine to hide. Perhaps somebody simply wanted to draw attention to themselves. Maybe owners of the theater, somewhere along the way, invented the story as a way of drawing in business.* It could be that some anxious hoofer or actor felt that old superstition at work and invented a ghost at the Lerner to make it easier to perform. No ghost, no show. So, voilà! A ghost is born.

Then again, it could well be that there really was an ill-fated technician who lingers on in the shadows. It would be nice to put a name to the face.

Theaters are places where dreams can come true in a single evening or be shattered in the blink of an eye. Those dreams don't always have to take place on a stage. A lighting booth or a spindly catwalk will do just fine.

---

* This, though, can be a double-edged sword. Think of a bed-and-breakfast, for example. Some people may be drawn to the prospect of spending a night in a haunted locale. Others would balk at the prospect and seek shelter elsewhere. How many people would be repelled by a haunted theater?

19

WHERE THE SPIRITS HAVE A BALL

Sometimes the origins of a ghost story are so bogged down in a quagmire of details that it's hard to sift through and find the truth. A case in point is the former State Farm office at 1307 Elkhart Road in Goshen. The squat brick building sits on a quarter-circle plot of land that has four different histories behind it. Now one lot, it consists of the remains of four separate lots that were eventually fused together. First platted on June 25, 1897, these four lots—and many more—composed the Hess West View Addition to the City of Goshen.

Lots 51, 52, 53 and 54 had different owners back in the mists of time, some more thoroughly documented than others. Indeed, the first record of anyone living on this tract of land is from 1922. Lewis and Minnie Miller were the first recorded residents of lots 51, 52 and 53. When they purchased the land is lost to history, at least according to the Elkhart County Registry Office. Records show they owned extensive tracts of land throughout Elkhart and the surrounding counties.

In 1922, the Millers sold the land to Howard and Daisy Heeter. Both were born in northern Indiana, and both would die in Florida after snowbirding it south to Clearwater. The Heeters are buried in Dade City, Florida. Interestingly, they had one child, a son they named Darwin Charles.

The Heeters sold lots 51 and 52 in 1929 to Irven Case and his wife, Hazel Ulrich Case. Irven and Hazel were both Indiana natives, like the Heeters, marrying in Goshen on June 12, 1912. Sometime after selling the land in

1944, they made their way to Los Angeles to live out their lives in sunny bliss. Both died in Los Angeles and are buried there.

In 1937, the City of Goshen decided to improve its infrastructure by paving what would become State Road 2—right through the Heeter property. The city approached Howard and Daisy and offered them the princely sum of $11.78 for a thin tract of land across lot 53. The Heeters took it.

More improvements came in 1938 with the building of U.S. 33, connecting St. Joseph, Michigan, with Richmond, Virginia—a scenic route that passed through Ohio and West Virginia, as well as the four lots in question. All four were reshaped and resized at this time, forming the curved side of the quarter-circle extant today. Shortly after, the Heeters sold what was left of lot 53 to Ward and Wanetah Sharp in 1938.

Hazel and Irven Case sold lots 51 and 52 to Father H.J. Miller in 1944, who immediately turned it over to Bishop (ultimately Archbishop) John Francis Noll of the Diocese of Fort Wayne, Indiana.

In addition to serving the Catholic Church for more than fifty years, Archbishop Noll was the author of *Father Smith Instructs Jackson*, a classic of Catholic literature published in 1948 and widely reprinted in the subsequent decades. Archbishop Noll was born in 1875 in Fort Wayne, where he eventually died in 1956. He is buried in Victory Noll Cemetery in Huntington, Indiana.

Archbishop Noll transferred his two lots in the Hess West View Addition to his successor, Bishop Pursley of Hartford City, Indiana, in 1949. Leo Aloysius Pursley was born on March 12, 1902. He attended St. Joseph College in Renssellaer, Indiana, and Mount Saint Mary Seminary in Cincinnati, Ohio. He passed away on November 11, 1998, in Fort Wayne, and is buried in Catholic Cemetery there.

Although the exact date is unknown, Bishop Pursley sold lots 51 and 52 to Margaret and Stephen Craig. Research on Findagrave and MyHeritage failed to locate any records for either, except to say that Margaret's maiden name was Baker. What makes this interesting is that lot 54 makes its first appearance in the records since its original platting back in 1897 as the property of Frances Baker, Amelia Baker (widow of John Baker), Florence B. Baker Defrees and her husband, Donald Defrees. Though there are no records to back it up, it is easy to conjecture that Frances, Florence, John and Margaret were closely related. Families often stuck together in the early part of the previous century, often living in adjacent houses, as may well be the case here.

In 1950, the Bakers and the Defreeses sold lot 54 to Ward and Wanetah Sharp, giving them two adjacent lots. (You'll recall that they purchased lot

53 in 1938.) In 1961, the Sharps acquired lots 51 and 52 from the Craigs, as well as lots 55, 56 and 57. Ward Sharp died in 1963 and was buried in Violett Cemetery in Goshen. Wanetah continued living on the property until 1984, when she sold lots 51 through 54 to Dr. Lawrence Falli and his wife, Kathleen. Wanetah continued living in Goshen until her death in 1989. She, too, is buried at Violett Cemetery.

Falli, a podiatrist, now in possession of the four lots, razed all the existing houses and constructed the squat brick pillbox that would serve as his office for the next two decades. Born on December 15, 1944, Falli retired in 2006 at the age of sixty-one. He and his wife relocated to Crown Point, Indiana. Dr. Falli passed away shortly after, on May 30, 2007, in Dyer, Indiana. His wife continues to live in Crown Point, where the doctor is buried.

Before moving, Falli sold the building to April Stewart Fryman, a State Farm agent. She ran her office until moving to Evansville, Indiana, in 2013. She, in turn, sold the property to Meridian Title, which operates out of the building today.

With the number of families that lived on these assorted lots over the years, there is a huge range of possibilities as to exactly who haunts the old State Farm office. All the families documented had children, most of them probably raised on this little pie-shaped piece of land. While there are no records to show who may have died on the property, let alone how, it is a good assumption that at least one of them did. It is quite possible that a child died. The following story lends credence to that theory.

Former State Farm office, where a team captured video of a ball moving of its own accord.

One of the most challenging aspects of ghost hunting is sorting fact from fiction—or, more specifically, fantasy. Perhaps that's being a bit cruel, as most people who report paranormal activity are convinced they are experiencing something genuine.

SPEAR (at that time including Jesse James, his wife, Matie, and me) investigated this office in 2012 at the invitation of Angie Michelson*, an agent in the office, and her colleague Robin Weiss* (both employees of April Stewart Fryman, who did not participate). The building is modern, spacious, bright and cheerful in every respect. The basement is finished to living-room perfection: lush, tan carpeting; soft sofas; a big-screen TV; and a long table covered in arts and crafts where Angie and Robin brought their children to play frequently. It is very inviting.

But the room also had a darker side, at least to Angie and Robin. In talking to them prior to our investigation, we discovered that the two young mothers, both in their early thirties, often gathered in the basement room to make popcorn and watch horror movies with the lights off. They claimed to feel the presence of another person in the room with them, to hear footsteps moving around upstairs and to see shadows passing down a back corridor, even in the middle of the day.

One hidden corridor, L-shaped, was located just off the basement room, behind a wooden door they always kept closed. Both Robin and Angie claimed to feel completely petrified in this dark passageway and refused to enter it unless absolutely necessary.

The inconvenient side of things, at least for SPEAR, was that they had no knowledge of who may be haunting the place. Certainly, no one had expired in the current building, at that time less than thirty years old and never a private home. They had a suspicion that it was a child, probably a boy, based on the selection of toys "he" chose to play with in the basement rec room. In particular, a small blue-and-white beach ball had a tendency to move about the room, even when Angie's and Robin's kids were not around.

Armed with this basic information and a bevy of equipment, including Jesse's DVR system, we gathered in the basement on a summer Saturday night. Robin set the beach ball in the middle of the conversation pit, and Jesse aimed a camera directly at it. Angie, Robin, Matie, Jesse and I spread ourselves around the circle of chairs and sofas surrounding the ball and began conducting a standard EVP session. All the while, the six-camera DVR system was recording the ball as well as other points on both levels of the office building, including the corridor that so unnerved Robin and Angie.

The room was dark and cool. It took a while for our eyes to adjust to the darkness. There was just enough light from the exit signs and a security light at the far end of the large room for us to make out each other and the beach ball. Everything seemed completely uneventful.

After about an hour, Jesse and I got up to investigate the L-shaped corridor. We took a digital recorder and an EMF detector. We spent about twenty minutes in the enclosed passageway, but neither of us felt the slightest unease. The digital recorder yielded no results when we played it back after the investigation. The EMF, on the other hand, gave us some startling results.

An EMF detector is a handheld device designed to detect electromagnetic fields. It is a common tool among electricians, which, like much ghost-hunting equipment, has been coopted to serve a new function. It is a matter of scientific fact that all living objects, as well as many inanimate objects, generate an electromagnetic field. That stands to reason, as all living things, from ants to zebras to State Farm agents, run on electricity. The whys and wherefores are beyond the purview of this book, but you can look it up in any high school biology textbook.

The only thing of note in the passageway was a computer mainframe—and what a doozy! Perched on a wide-open shelf, this colossus of technology was pumping out an EMF in excess of 200 milligauss! A human body averages an output of less than 0.1 milligauss. Anyone who has watched TV shows like *Ghost Hunters* or studied paranormal investigation knows that high electromagnetic fields can cause any number of symptoms, including nausea, dizziness, paranoia, hallucinations, skin rashes and fatigue. Angie and Robin certainly identified feelings of fear, perhaps paranoia, caused by the enormous amount of energy that computer was pumping out.

We suggested they put some kind of box around the computer tower to contain the EMF. Wood, metal or plastic would do the job and would most likely reduce the feelings they were experiencing. To the best of my knowledge, they never did.

Having discovered the probable cause of their discomfort, Jesse and I tried to persuade Robin and Angie to join us in the passageway so we could demonstrate our findings. Both refused point-blank to enter the hallway. They also were skeptical of our findings. Unfortunately, without them beside us to view the EMF detector, we could do little to convince them of our discovery.

The investigation was still only partly complete, so we returned to the circle of chairs gathered around the beach ball. Remember, our DVR camera was pointed directly at the ball, and all of our feet were visible in the shot. We continued talking among ourselves and throwing the occasional question out into the ether, but the atmosphere in the room was very congenial and comfortable. But we continued on, watching the ball.

Sure enough, after a while and a little prompting, we could all see the ball moving on its own. They were small movements, little more than rocking back and forth most of the time, but it did eventually describe a complete circle about five inches in diameter. Being naturally skeptical, I began looking around for vents, but there were none anywhere near. The only two air vents were in the ceiling at opposite ends of the large room, nowhere near the conversation pit and the beach ball. The air-conditioning was on during the whole of the evening, but it was not nearly powerful enough to move that ball, especially in a complete circle.

The DVR, which we watched right there before closing up for the night, clearly showed the ball teetering back and forth for several minutes before making an unmistakable circular movement. Even that took several minutes to complete, as it moved, unprompted, in little fits and starts. As mentioned, our feet were clearly visible on the screen, so it was obvious that no one touched the ball or pushed it with any part of their body. Blowing on it would have been impossible to conceal, as the camera would have picked up the sound as well as the image. Any trickster's attempts at sabotage would have been spotted immediately.

In the end, we could offer Angie and Robin no explanations. They refused to accept our findings about the computer in the back passageway, and we were at a loss to explain the rolling ball. I did recommend that they experiment by altering the tone of their movie nights to see if it would make a difference. We suggested that they try *Toy Story* or *Shakespeare in Love* instead of the ghost stories and gory slasher movies they loved. It's possible that their taste in movies, combined with the feelings of paranoia and of being watched, were preconditioning them to believe in the presence of ghosts in the office. If you go into an allegedly haunted location expecting to see ghosts, you're already halfway toward seeing one. The power of suggestion is undeniable, but it can be controlled.

As far as I am aware, they never took my advice on the movies, either. Repeated attempts to get in contact with Angie and Robin since the investigation have failed, so there is no way to verify whether or not they altered their routine.

Is the former State Farm office in Goshen haunted? There is definitely something unusual going on. How else to explain a beach ball that moves around with no human assistance? But is that enough to say the place is haunted?

Not long after completing this investigation, Angie invited us to investigate her home in nearby White Pigeon, Michigan. There we found ample evidence of spirit activity, which makes me wonder if the ghost in the office may be attached to Angie directly. Could she have been transporting a ghost back and forth to work every day? It's unlikely, but stranger things have happened.

20

THAT OL' SCHOOL SPIRIT

Just as every high school allegedly has a ghost or two, every college campus can also boast of its own paranormal legends. Indeed, entire books have been written on that campus spirit, if you'll pardon the pun. My own alma mater, Hartwick College in Oneonta, New York, claims the legend of former president Willard Yager setting fire to the building that now bears his name. Students claim to see Yager starting the blaze, although why he should do so is never explained. The building in question did not even exist when Yager was president, so why should he bear a grudge against it?

Goshen College was founded in 1894 as the Elkhart Institute of Science, Industry and the Arts. The Mennonite Church eventually took over and, in 1903, convinced the directors to relocate the campus a few miles south to the growing town of Goshen. The school acquired a tract of land on the Abraham Shoup farm in June of that year. The new location conveniently sat beside a railroad, allowing students to travel to the new campus from wherever they hailed.

Umble Hall, built in 1978 as a performing arts center, claims two ghosts dwelling within its brown-stone walls. The building was named for John Umble, an English professor at Goshen for many years.

John Sylvanus Umble was born in Kelly Point, Pennsylvania, on February 16, 1881, the son of Benjamin Franklin and Nancy Stoltzfus Umble and the oldest of five. His father's family had strong ties to Ohio, and John would spend much of his life there. His early years remain obscure, but the story starts to flesh out in the twentieth century. He was one of the first graduates of the Elkhart Institute of Science, Industry and the Arts, a connection that he would maintain for decades.

He married Alice Landis of Sterling, Illinois, on Christmas Day 1906 in Elkhart. John and Alice had two sons, Roy and B. Frank Umble. Roy was born in Ohio in 1913, indicating that the family had relocated there sometime before then. A passport application dated February 19, 1910, indicates that the family was living in Akron at the time. John Umble listed his occupation as "teacher," though many existing records tag him as a "principal." Of what remains unknown, at least in online records.

John enlisted in the U.S. Army on September 12, 1918. His military registration card lists him as being short and of medium build. Indeed, his passport application lists his height as five feet, seven inches. At the time of his enlistment, he was working as a farmer in West Liberty, Ohio.

Throughout the 1930s, John Umble authored a number of newspaper articles about the Mennonites, particularly their schools. At least two books followed: *Ohio Mennonite Sunday Schools*, published in 1941, and *Goshen College, 1894–1954*, published by the college in 1955.

He joined the faculty of Goshen College as an English and speech professor in 1925, staying on the job for more than a quarter century, retiring in 1951. During that time, he helped introduce theater arts to the curriculum. At the time, Goshen College had no theater, so classes and rehearsals were conducted in a number of locations, a difficult situation that only emphasized the need for a permanent theater arts building. That vision would not come true until 1978, twelve years after John Umble's death on November 14, 1966, in Archbold, Ohio. He and Alice, who died in 1969, are both buried in Violett Mennonite Cemetery in Goshen.

Students and faculty at Umble Hall report the traditional symptoms of a haunting. Lights turn on and off of their own accord. Objects fall from the flies and clatter onto the stage below. Eerie sounds resonate from the catwalks high above the boards. Whether any of these phenomena can be attributed to John Umble remains uncertain.

A female ghost, dubbed "Alice," after John's wife, has also been reported in the theater arts building.

Even though Umble Hall did not exist at the time of his death, it's not hard to see why John might choose to haunt the building named for him. All those years of trudging from one place to another just to mount a production would have been frustrating. Perhaps he enjoys finally having a permanent home in which to practice his craft. And what better way to spend eternity than with your beloved wife at your side?

21

NIGHT SHIFT

Thousands of old factories, mills and other industrial buildings around the country have been renovated into apartments, studios, shopping malls, hotels, museums and other venues beneficial to the surrounding community. Most of these buildings have rich, storied histories. Some of them still harbor workers whose shifts ended decades, maybe even centuries, ago. Yet they continue to trudge the floors of their old workplaces, determined to get the job done.

The Old Bag Factory in Goshen is one of the lucky ones. Time and civic pride have given this venerable building a new lease on life. Today, it is a quaint collection of shops and artisan studios displaying handcrafted furniture, pottery and other delights for the discerning shopper. It also features a Mexican restaurant and an escape room (by appointment only).

Located at 1100 North Chicago Avenue, a stretch of the nationally treasured Lincoln Highway, this 1896 brown-brick structure started out life as the Cosmo Buttermilk Soap factory. The brainchild of Ohio-born entrepreneur J.J. Burns (there are no records to tell us what the J.J. stood for), Cosmo Buttermilk Soap was a leader in the Victorian soap trade. The firm also manufactured toilet paper.

The hulking building consists of more than eighty thousand square feet on four levels. Original beechwood beams, painted white, supported the floors, tapering in thickness as they rose toward the soaring roof. Burns built a freestanding, coal-fired power plant immediately adjacent to the factory.

The Old Bag Factory, where three workers died on duty, including one who fell into a vat of asphalt.

Thick leather belts drove the machinery in the factory, powered by the steam-generating furnaces in the power plant. A railroad spur led down a gentle slope alongside the factory to allow products to be shipped all over the United States.

According to Goshen historian Raymond Jorgenson, Burns—a civil engineer by training—designed the railroad line that linked Shipshewana, Indiana, to White Pigeon, Michigan, just above the state line, and, eventually, to Goshen. The Cosmo spur was linked directly to this line.

The power plant was a marvel of efficiency, producing a generous excess of power, more than the factory itself needed. Ever the entrepreneur, Burns applied this surplus to running a trolley that snaked its way through Goshen, starting at the Cosmo Buttermilk Soap factory. It wound back and forth down the middle of city streets, eventually reaching a turntable about halfway down Eighth Street, where it would retrace its path.

Burns also designed the historic Pennsylvania truss bridge across the Elkhart River, immediately across Chicago Avenue from the Old Bag Factory parking lot, to accommodate those trolley cars. The bridge, with a weight limit of a staggering thirteen tons when most such bridges were limited to one ton, was a marvel in its own right, designed to rock back and forth on rollers to keep the heavy trolley cars from tearing it apart.

In addition to his clever engineering skills, Burns was an apt negotiator. He agreed to build his factory on farmland outside what was then the town of Goshen. The town agreed to provide Burns and his factory with city water and electricity if he, in turn, agreed to develop the area into a subdivision for his workers to reside close to work. Thus, the city got a generous expansion of its boundaries as well as a bevy of new utility customers. It was a win-win situation for everyone.

By 1910, however, the Cosmo Buttermilk Soap Factory had run its course. The building was sold to the Chicago-Detroit Bag Company, which renovated the structure, adding cream-brick towers to each corner—one story taller than the rest of the building. These soaring towers, devoid of floors inside, were used to dry enormous lengths of newly dyed fabric before it was made into bags. These towers have since been lowered to roof height.

Under the name Chase Bag Factory (one of twenty-two facilities Chase owned across the country), the company produced many different types of bags, including burlap potato sacks, cloth onion bags and even waterproof sandbags for the military.

"I met a man from Massachusetts," Raymond says with an amused smile. "And what his job was, he called on textile mills because of the big looms they used to shuttle the threads back and forth with a big boom." It was this man's duty to calibrate each loom so that it would shuttle at a different time from the others. "If all the looms hit at the same time, the building would fall to pieces."

Starting in 1921, Chase contracted with the Hershey chocolate company to manufacture, of all things, the little white paper "flags" that pop out of the foil of Hershey's Kisses. The factory in Goshen continued to produce these flags for more than sixty years. Each month, a boxcar-load of flags (also called plumes) weighing 45,000 pounds was shipped to Hershey, Pennsylvania.

"They brought a big paper-slitting machine up from Louisiana," Raymond says. Huge rolls of paper were cut into tiny two-inch-long strips that were then shipped off to Hershey to be wrapped in foil along with the familiar candy treat.

In the early 1920s, Chase executives coined the term *bagology* to elevate the bag-making process to a science. Today, visitors to the building can still see the word emblazoned across the brick exterior facing the old iron bridge.

A contract with the U.S. military to produce sandbags became a lifesaver for the company in the twentieth century, fueling production to new heights during the two world wars. During these periods, the Chase Bag Factory was one of the largest employers in Elkhart County, with up to one thousand workers filling its three shifts seven days a week.

"My wife's grandmother, mother and father all worked there," Raymond says. "This was the place you wanted to work."

Raymond's wife, Rose Marie, reminisces about her family. "The plant was unionized. It was the Textile Workers' Union of America. My mother was the first secretary-treasurer of the union. She had to leave the job when I came along in 1946." In those days, pregnant women were not encouraged to work, particularly in dangerous environments such as factories. Massive machinery, driven by exposed belts on enormous drive wheels, were notorious for their ability to grab hold of loose clothing. Maiming and other injuries were often fatal.

Rose Marie's mother was replaced by a man named Ed Kyle, who served as secretary-treasurer until his death, at which point her father assumed this role. He worked in this capacity until the factory closed in 1982. Among his accomplishments was ensuring that Chase workers received a pension, something most factories had done away with by that time.

As it was, the factory did endure two strikes in the twentieth century. History is sketchy on these strikes, but according to the Jorgensons, the first lasted just a weekend, the workers declaring a freeze on Friday evening. By Monday morning, they were all back to work, their demands having been met swiftly by management. A second strike didn't fare so well, lasting several weeks.

In a demonstration of their determination, strikers greased the rails on the factory's inclined spur. When the train arrived to drop off large rolls of paper from which the little flags were made, the engine's wheels could not gain purchase, and the train slid all the way to the bottom of the spur. Unable to get up again, it had to be pulled back up onto the main track.

Rose Marie laughs about one particular memory. "Much to the chagrin of the management, they had to have facilities for the strikers who were walking the beat, and so they put Port-a-Potties out there. They were really embarrassed about that!"

Raymond recounts a particularly hair-raising memory. The machinery for the factory was oiled constantly to keep it running smoothly. That oil would dribble down into pools on the basement floor. In order to clean the floors, maintenance personnel would ignite gasoline to burn the grease off. "It's amazing it's still there," he says of the huge old structure.

In the earliest days of the factory, the machinery was steam-driven. Large coal furnaces were kept fed by teams of horses stabled on the property.

Raymond points out how, as the horses died off, they were buried in a large mound next to the factory. The mound is still visible today.

The Chase Bag Factory finally closed its doors in 1982. The building sat empty for two years before being purchased by Larion and Nancy Swartzendruber. By this time, the building was infested with birds and rodents, the woodwork was rotting and the locally made bricks were crumbling. Much hard work brought the derelict hulk back to a newfound glory. Today, the Old Bag Factory is a unique tourist attraction, drawing travelers looking for one-of-a-kind and beautiful things for their homes.

But not everything in the building is new. According to Raymond Jorgenson, at least three ghosts are believed to walk the floors of the Old Bag Factory. "Three workers were killed out there in accidents. They used to have, where the porch is now for the restaurant, a big asphalt tank in there [for the waterproof sandbags], and they had one guy fall into the tank. Two others died over the years in the factory. So people who work at night say they always hear weird noises. Well, the building's 130 years old. You get weird noises anyway."

Even if Raymond and Rose Marie Jorgenson do not believe in the spirits of the Old Bag Factory, there are plenty who do. So, the next time you're in Goshen on a shopping expedition, stop by the Old Bag Factory. Have lunch at the Mexican restaurant, browse through the shops and displays (a local model railroad club has a jaw-dropping layout on the second floor) and take in the history. Informational signs dot the walls, identifying and explaining original pieces of equipment poised around the building. You might not hear the mysterious footsteps during the day, but if you can wrangle a visit in the nighttime hours, you just might get more than you bargained for.

22

THE MAN IN THE RED FLANNEL SHIRT

Few people would deny that being locked up in jail is one of the most traumatic things a human can encounter. Only recently have jails and their more stalwart counterparts, prisons, become places of rehabilitation, giving inmates an opportunity to reflect and repent for their misdeeds. But this was not always so. Prisons, such as the notorious Alcatraz in San Francisco Bay, California, were designed for one purpose: punishment.

But, just as the punishment must fit the crime, the facility must fit the town. For that reason, the original Elkhart County Jail, constructed in 1879 in downtown Goshen, was little more than a reinforced home. Built out of brick in the Italianate style, the original county jail served as more than a restraining facility. It was also the sheriff's home. Early county sheriffs and their families lived in the jail alongside the usual weekend suspects and the occasional long-haul prisoner. Often, the sheriff's wife would cook meals for the inmates. Designed to accommodate no more than a dozen prisoners at any given time, this old structure served its purpose for an amazing amount of time, remaining active until its demolition in 1972.

Two years before, the county began discussing the need for a newer, larger, more modern facility. Located at 114 North Second Street in Goshen, the new structure, officially dubbed the Elkhart County Police & Security Center, was to be the absolute state-of-the-art in jails. Equipped with electronic locks that even the police officers needed a security check to pass

Original Elkhart County Jail, built in 1879. *Courtesy of Indiana Landmarks, Wilbur D. Peat Collection.*

through, as well as a building-wide closed-circuit TV (CCTV) system, the new jail, constructed between 1970 and 1972, also served as the emergency dispatch center for Goshen police, fire and ambulance services. The facility was equipped with voice-recognition technology to detect the guilty in the event of a fraudulent emergency call. There was even an early version of the internet—a computer hookup to virtually every police office, jail and prison in the United States.

The new building was a solid block of brick and concrete, four stories tall and formidable, with very few windows looking out over the city. Concern for security took precedence over aesthetics. Originally intended to house a maximum of 150 inmates, by 1981, the building was already overcrowded. Increasing crime in the 1980s did nothing to relieve the situation. By 1985, an extension was underway, to be opened officially on August 10, 1986.

One of the most embarrassing incidents in the jail's history occurred just two nights later. The inmates were to be relocated to the new addition while upgrades were made to the original building. Unfortunately, the population was still greater than the available capacity of the new wing, so the warden

The 1972 Elkhart County Jail, where several inmates saw the ghost of an unidentified man. *Courtesy of WNDU TV.*

at the time opted to house prisoners in three third-floor cells that had not yet been completed. Steel crossbars over the windows were conspicuously absent, as were toilets.

Six juvenile inmates were housed in these rooms. They immediately began planning their escape. The lack of security in the rooms made escape all but guaranteed. Using a pipe torn loose from the incomplete plumbing, the youths forced a window away from its frame. In true jailbreak fashion, they made a rope out of bedsheets and lowered themselves from the window. Like something out of a Peter Sellers comedy, their rope dangled just inches from a security camera rendered moot by the fact that outdoor security lighting had not yet been installed. If it wasn't for an alert communications officer, Dolores Jill Wilkins*, monitoring the CCTV system, they might have been able to scamper away into the dark night. As it was, they were rounded up almost immediately.

News of the foiled escape attempt leaked out, embarrassing the sheriff of the day, who took full responsibility for the failure of the jail's security systems. He ran again for office but was not reelected.

There were other embarrassments at the Elkhart County Jail. Many of the doors inside did not have functioning electronic locks, while others were missing keys. Plumbing on the upper levels leaked prodigiously, flooding offices on the ground floor. Ceiling tiles collapsed, and carpets were soaked under inches of water. Also, by 1986, the concrete exterior was beginning to show streaks of rust from the dissolving rebar inside. Never a slave to beauty, the ugly block was becoming an eyesore in the community. Maintenance costs proved prohibitive as time went on, and by 1990, the county had chosen to build a new facility. Located in the current Elkhart County Corrections Center, the current jail, completed in 1992, is a marvel of architecture and function, putting its predecessor to shame.

Still, the old hulk endured. Abandoned, the jail became—ironically—a hangout for teenagers and the homeless. Situated directly across Second Street from the beautiful, historic Goshen Courthouse, the concrete monstrosity was rotting and crumbling, posing a physical danger as well as being unsightly. Plans for its demolition floundered in bureaucracy for an additional twenty-seven years. It was finally torn down in 2019. The lot sits empty beside the oldest house in Goshen, now an attorney's office.

As for the ghost of the old Elkhart County Jail, there really isn't much to tell. No public records exist to tell how many people may have died in the building (let alone the original jail, which stood for ninety-three years) or who they were. However, at least one soul survived the ultimate judgment to linger in the ugly box on Second Street.

Sheriff's Deputy Rodden Gehringer* recalled working in the jail one night in the late 1980s. It had been a peaceful evening overall, and he was just relaxing before his next patrol of the cellblocks. All of a sudden, screams, loud and piercing, issued from the women's cellblock. Gehringer rushed to investigate. On reaching the cellblock, he found several female inmates in a state of panic. When he asked why, more than one woman reported seeing a man in a red-plaid work shirt standing in the corridor outside the cells. They told him the man had simply materialized in front of them and then disappeared just as suddenly when they screamed.

Gehringer initiated a thorough search of the facility, both men's and women's blocks, but found no one out of their cell or wandering the building. Besides, the inmates did not wear red-plaid shirts. The women were unable to give a good description of the man, as he appeared to be transparent. Who he may have been is anybody's guess. Perhaps he had served time in the jail. But why would he be in the women's block? Women were allowed visitors, but not in the cellblock. Could he have worked at the jail in the past? Maybe, but staff members wore traditional khaki uniforms, not red-flannel shirts.

It has been more than twenty years since Gehringer worked in the old Elkhart County Jail, and this was his one and only encounter with the paranormal. He could recall no other stories from the many years he served in the jail. He is still active with the sheriff's department today. To the best of his knowledge, no one else saw the man in plaid. Since the building is now two years gone, it is unlikely anyone will know the man's identity or his purpose in showing up one night all those years ago. If any teens or homeless persons encountered this spirit in the decaying jail, their stories have not come to light.

Then again, like most prison stories, it might be better to leave this one in the past.

23

A Hole in Space and Time

Sometimes, a haunted location is not what it appears to be.

Ox Bow Park, located along the Elkhart River at the point where Goshen and Dunlap meet, is a beautiful wilderness full of hiking trails, picnic spots, observation towers and enough wildlife to keep John James Audubon sketching for years. Comprising over 113 acres of fields and marshland, Ox Bow Park offers a year-round selection of programs and opportunities for the outdoor enthusiast. Admission is minimal, free if you're on foot or on a bicycle.

But what you may not know is that this park used to be a farm. More specifically, it was the Elkhart County Home, a place where the indigent could live and work in a safe and respectful environment. In addition to the poor, it also housed the mentally ill, orphans and the elderly. It was just one of many such facilities in the national County Farm system developed in the mid-1800s.

This particular tract of land was originally settled by Alexander and Jane Frier McConaughy. Jane was the daughter of James Frier, an Irish immigrant who served as the first county assessor. He was forced to give up his job because he was not a naturalized citizen.

Alexander and Jane had a son named Charles, born in 1851 in Iowa. He and his wife, Ellen Reed, raised five children on the family farm in Goshen. He and Ellen offered land to the county to build the Elkhart County Home. They continued living on the edges of the property. Charles died of a

Elkhart County Home, where long-dead children still laugh and cry. *Courtesy of* Goshen News.

cerebral hemorrhage on March 3, 1939, in Elkhart. Alexander and Jane are buried in the McConaughy Cemetery. Charles and his entire family are buried in Jackson Township Cemetery in Benton.

Charles's son Leonard inherited the property around the county home, selling it to D. Blanch Struble by 1956. Struble sold the land to the Elkhart Parks Department in 1969.

Constructed in 1886, the Elkhart County Home, a sprawling Gothic Revival structure in white brick, originally consisted of 113 rooms. The surrounding acreage featured alfalfa fields, barns, a pen for hogs, storage buildings and other farm support facilities. Residents of the county home worked the land, helped raise the crops and livestock and assisted in the sale of the crops to local merchants in exchange for room, board and medical care. The home itself even featured a beauty salon. Residents were treated with dignity and respect, the home being officially recognized as one of the best and most efficient in the country. At its peak, the Elkhart County Home housed 116 inmates, as they were called.

The heyday of the County Farm system was short-lived. With the coming of the twentieth century, the private healthcare industry began to mushroom. Existing staff members were not trained to deal with new medical technologies. The inflow of new patients for the county home fell to a trickle. The facility managed to lumber on until 1967, when proceedings commenced for its closure. The surrounding farmland was deeded to the county for the formation of Ox Bow Park, named for the large, looping lake, a former meander of the Elkhart River, in its acreage.

Efforts to save Elkhart County Home were fierce. In particular, Elkhart County councilwoman Marjory Madlem formed a group called Home Sweet Home. For nearly a decade, Madlem and her team fought the county through petitions, lawsuits and a referendum. All efforts failed in turn, and the last residents were finally relocated to alternative facilities in 1977.

The hulking structure, now sitting in the midst of a county park, remained standing, empty, for another four years. It was finally razed in 1981. All that remains is a small historic marker, the memories of local residents, two wildly overgrown cemeteries and the stories.

And there are stories. Nothing concrete, if you'll forgive the pun, but rumors do persist of spooky goings-on in the park. Several paranormal investigation teams have scrutinized the area with their gadgets over the years, but little in the way of solid evidence has manifested. Generally, people speak of eerie feelings, as if they're being watched. Whispered voices, the crying and laughter of children (at night in a park that closes at sundown) and shadow figures have all been reported over the years.

The old McConaughy family cemetery has yielded some EVPs, but the nearby Elkhart County Home Cemetery seems peaceful enough. Much of the activity in the vicinity is attributed to the Elkhart River. Moving water has long been regarded as a catalyst for paranormal activity.

But can a river draw extraterrestrials? Perhaps the strangest occurrence reported from Ox Bow Park happened in 1973. Police received reports of a bluish disc or orb hovering over the park. Newspaper clippings indicate that it disappeared somewhere near Bristol, a considerable distance from the park. One officer filed a report of his own sighting in Ox Bow, claiming the object he saw was greenish-yellow. It disappeared before his eyes. No logical explanation has ever been found.

Today, Ox Bow Park, just off U.S. Highway 33 between Elkhart and Goshen, is a peaceful, soothing place at any time of year. Summer soccer games give way to cross-country skiing. The park is open during daylight hours only, so you will need permission to be inside the grounds after the sun sets. If you do venture out there, however, keep your eyes and ears open. While the old Elkhart County Home no longer exists and the two cemeteries are difficult to find on the sunniest of days, some of the residents may still be hanging around, just waiting for the chance to tell their own stories.

24

FOUR STORIES, NO ANSWERS

CABLE LINE ROAD, JIMTOWN

Sometimes, a story is just a story, with little factual evidence to back it up. Such is the case of the Cable Line Road Monster in rural Jamestown, known locally as Jimtown, a few lonely miles south of Elkhart.

There are at least four stories of how this particular haunt came into being. All involve a fatal crash at the rural intersection of County Road 26 (Cable Line Road) and County Road 11. The first version tells of a motorcyclist racing hell-bent down Cable Line Road at night some time "in the 1960s" and losing control, slamming into a tree. The force of the impact decapitated the young biker. According to the story, he hit the tree face-first with such power that his likeness was embedded in the bark of the tree for all eternity.

Reports tell that a headless figure in a black leather jacket and boots can occasionally be seen walking along Cable Line Road, looking for his head. Some people say his head will appear on the hood of your car, staring at you as you try to get away. This version also claims that, if you stop your car at this intersection, you will not be able to start it again before the headless biker reaches you.

The second version claims it was a car, not a motorcycle, that lost control at the intersection on a dark autumn night, plowing into the tree. The driver was thrown clean through the windshield, losing his head in the process. As in the first story, the head struck the tree trunk with enough force to imprint the man's visage in the bark. The story goes on to state that the man's head was found, but not the rest of his body. Again, a headless man is seen walking west along County Road 26. This legend adds that the man's spirit tries to escape from the tree every Halloween night.

A third version, the **only** one to give anything close to a specific date for the crash—1958—says there were two cars involved. The cars, carrying a combined total of five people, collided with each other at this fateful junction. Two people, including the driver, were thrown from one of the vehicles. Again, the driver flew through the windshield, which severed his head from his body. The passenger survived to tell the tale.

Finally, a fourth version claims that a lone driver was racing down Cable Line Road in his sports car one foggy night when he saw a pickup truck speeding toward him up County Road 11. With two drivers rushing at each other, both apparently oblivious of the other until it was too late, a crash was inevitable. The young sportster was pitched from his car and thrown against the tree, where his body—but *not* his head—left a lasting impression. This story also says the driver's head will appear on the hood of your car as you pass by his death site.

In classic urban legend style, a Jimtown teenager heard the story of a young couple parked alongside Cable Line Road on a dark, foggy night when they were startled by a loud, scraping noise on the outside of the car. Further investigation revealed long, deep scratches in the paint, as if made by sharp claws. Could this explain why the ghost is referred to as a monster?

This same story—typed up but never published, bearing no author's name and now housed in the files of the Elkhart County Historical Society in Bristol—recounts the legend of the motorcyclist, but it also claims that the tree bleeds on the anniversary of his death. Unfortunately, it does not specify when that anniversary is.

Further from this account, a green fog is said to shroud the handful of bridges along Cable Line Road and that a troll lives beneath one of them. If you stop your car on this bridge, the troll will get you. The fog itself manifests at random times of the day and night and is accompanied by six-legged creatures and other deformities frolicking about in the abutting cornfields.

No matter which version you subscribe to, the one thing they all have in common is that the image of the dead man can be seen in the bark of the tree. There is a phenomenon known in paranormal investigating circles as matrixing—the mind's attempt to make sense out of randomness. One of the most common examples is seeing faces in leaves, in stone, in clouds, just about anywhere. Low lighting and a chance triangular positioning of holes, spots or other visible items can fool the eye into seeing a face. (See the photograph reproduced in chapter 11.) A receptive mind can do the rest, especially if one is in a location believed to be haunted.

A number of things make these stories questionable. First, not one of them records the name of the victim. Second, only one of them gives a date, and even that is limited to the year. Another vaguely refers to an entire decade. Third, one legend claims that the haunting occurs only on Halloween. There's your big clue right there!

On the other hand, an article in the *Elkhart Truth* of August 18, 1958, tells of a real accident at this lonely junction. Two cars did, indeed, collide in 1958—but the fatality was that of a woman. Sophia Kazda of South Bend, Indiana, age forty-five, was in the passenger seat when her husband, George, ran a stop sign and T-boned another car. Kazda's 1956 Plymouth plowed head-first into the tree, ejecting both Sophia and George. The other car, a 1952 Nash driven by sixteen-year-old Keith Cook, spun out, reversed and collided again with the Plymouth.

Here's the rub. While George Kazda was thrown clear of both vehicles, sustaining non-life-threatening injuries, poor Sophia was flung in such a way that she landed half inside the Nash, sustaining massive head injuries. The two cars had to be pulled apart by a tow truck in order to free Sophia's body from the wreckage. She died at a local hospital approximately three hours after the crash. Cook and his two teenage passengers suffered minor cuts but nothing more.

So that adds a historic, if conflicting, note to the legend. Undoubtedly, there was a fatal crash at this intersection in 1958, but the victim was not a biker, not a man at all. However, the fact that Mrs. Kazda sustained severe head wounds might account for a headless ghost. But how could a middle-aged woman dressed in 1950s clothing be mistaken for a man, let alone a leather-clad biker? The *Truth* article, published just hours after the accident, naturally makes no mention of a ghost.

Another fatal accident, undocumented as far as I can tell, occurred in 2009. An unnamed woman lost control and plowed her vehicle into a telephone pole, dying instantly. The story does not recount the cause of the crash, but many attribute it to an appearance of the monster.

The legend of the Cable Line Road Monster is so beloved in Jimtown that the locals actually feature him (it?) on a parade float each year!

Today, there are no signs bearing the name Cable Line Road. This lonely stretch of macadam, surrounded by farmland on both sides and dotted with occasional houses, is quiet at the best of times. On a desolate, rainy day, as

Cable Line Road and County Road 11, haunted by an accident victim for more than seventy years. Cable Line Road runs across the picture.

seen in the photo reproduced here, it is not hard to imagine looking eastward and seeing a headless apparition groping its way toward you.

The ominous tree, bearing the visage of a long-dead motorist, was felled in 1994, so no one will see that eerie spectacle again. Why the tree was cut down is unclear. An *Elkhart Truth* article told of the accursed tree's felling but blamed it on disease. Could the tree have been causing traffic snarls as curious rubberneckers stopped to examine it? Unlikely. County Roads 11 and 26 are well outside Elkhart and Goshen city limits and are lightly traveled today. It is hard to imagine they'd be jammed back in 1958, even by morbid gawkers.

A classic urban legend, told from four different perspectives, with additional monsters thrown in for good measure. Is anyone right? You'll have to drive down Cable Line Road one Halloween night and find out for yourself—if you dare.

25

THE CRYING STONE

UNION CENTER CEMETERY, NEAR NAPPANEE

N o cemetery would be complete without a weeping gravestone. Indeed, there are probably hundreds of examples of crying stones around the world.

One such graveyard, Union Center Cemetery, also known as Pippenger Cemetery, is located just east of rural Nappanee, Indiana, in the southern portion of Elkhart County, at the corner of County Road 11 and County Road 50.

This part of Elkhart County is peppered with many small cemeteries, ranging from ancient and weather-worn to modern and sleek. Indeed, this portion of Elkhart County seems more dead than alive! Union Center falls somewhere in between the old and the new, blending early graves, including a small patch on the east side of County Road 11, with newer graves as you move westward.

The story concerns the grave of one Irwin Yoder (November 25, 1879–November 9, 1903). Yoder is one of the most common surnames in northern Indiana, particularly in Elkhart and LaGrange Counties. In fact, there are no fewer than twelve Yoders buried at Union Center.

Irwin's grave practically overhangs the retaining wall along County Road 11, virtually all that keeps the poor chap from spilling into oncoming traffic.

Above: Irwin Yoder's gravestone, which weeps over the damage inflicted by vandals.

Opposite: Closeup of Irwin Yoder's grave, showing the damage to his portrait.

Records of Irwin's life are scant. He was the son of John D. Yoder (1846–1893) and Catherine Iffert Yoder (1843–1922). He was the youngest of three children, preceded by sister Eliza and brother Edward. Barely out of his teens at the time of his death, Irwin was unmarried and left no descendants. What he did for a living is not recorded. Most likely, he worked on the family farm.

At any rate, the legend of the weeping tombstone states that, at some point in the twentieth century, unknown vandals, probably bent on getting some kicks in this otherwise sleepy hamlet, invaded Union Center Cemetery and took a hammer to Irwin's gravestone, striking his image just below the eye. The stone has been said to cry ever since.

Discoloration just below Irwin's eye does resemble tears. Could Irwin Yoder be weeping over the desecration of his final resting place? Alas, no records indicate who the miscreants were or what became of them, assuming they were ever identified in the first place.

Irwin's stone is engraved with a rather ironic poem, given the circumstances:

Farewell, Dear Friends, From Thee I Am Gone.
My Sufferings Now Are O'er.
My Friends Who Knew And Loved Me,
Will Know Me Here No More.

It would appear his epitaph is only half right. The poor young man, who died just sixteen days shy of his twenty-fourth birthday, has apparently not seen the last of his sufferings. If the story is to be believed, he is in anguish to this very day. If you seek out his eternal home, it may be fitting to weep a tear of your own to help ease young Irwin's grief.

CONCLUSION

So there you have a sampling of the spooky history of just one of Indiana's ninety-two counties. No doubt the others can offer an equally satisfying survey of the supernatural. Whether you believe in ghosts, monsters, aliens, UFOs or ESP doesn't really matter. Each person views the world in a unique way, and that will never change. The important thing is to keep an open mind to the possibilities.

Science has made wonderful strides in explaining how germs work and how radio waves operate. We can replace a heart or a cornea and send the patient home in a matter of days, if not hours. We launch vehicles that travel to the outer limits of the solar system and talk back to us, telling us of their adventures in space. Some of us even live in outer space on a limited basis.

Why, then, is it so hard to prove the existence of ghosts? Some might say that God, or whatever higher power you believe in, does not want us to know the truth. And I'm not sure I want to know, either. I'm of English descent, and any Agatha Christie fan will tell you the English love a good mystery. Besides, would life be nearly as colorful if we knew how everything worked? I don't think so. Part of what makes it exciting is the quest to find the answers. Whether we ever do is irrelevant. It's the search that counts. They say getting there is half the fun.

This book is just the tip of the proverbial iceberg. The first written encounter with a ghost comes from ancient Phoenicia, more than 3,400 years ago. The first documented paranormal investigation was conducted by

Pliny the Younger in AD 101. That's three and a half millennia of eyewitness accounts. A full dossier of the world's haunts would weigh almost as much as earth itself. The evidence is there, whether science can dissect it or not. Choose for yourself. I, for one, am only too glad to continue exploring.

About the Author

Selfie of the author at work.

Mark Doddington was born in Silver Spring, Maryland, in 1968, and raised in Laurel, Maryland. He graduated from Hartwick College in Oneonta, New York, in 1990 with a BA in creative writing and American literature. He currently lives in the 1903 Wilson Wilbert Wilt House in Elkhart, Indiana, and works as membership coordinator, among other things, at Ruthmere Museum, one block from his home. He is the editor and designer of *Robert Recalls: A Collection of Essays Written for the Ruthmere Record from 2003–2020*, by Robert Beardsley, published by Ruthmere Museum. He has also written three novels, two plays, several short stories and more than seventy songs, all unpublished. *Haunted Elkhart County* is his first published book as an author.

Visit us at
www.historypress.com